Better Homes and Gardens®

CHRISTMAS COOKING
FROM THE HEART™

Meredith® Books
Des Moines, Iowa

Our seal assures you that every recipe in *Christmas Cooking from the Heart*™ 2004 has been tested in the Better Homes and Gardens® Test Kitchen. This means that each recipe is practical and reliable, and meets our high standards of taste appeal. We guarantee your satisfaction with this book for as long as you own it.

All of us at Meredith® Books are dedicated to providing you with information and ideas to enhance your home. We welcome your comments and suggestions. Write to us at: Meredith Books, Food and Crafts Editorial Department, 1716 Locust St., Des Moines, IA 50309-3023. *Christmas Cooking from the Heart*™ is available by mail. To order past editions from past years, call 800/627-5490.

If you would like to purchase any of our cooking, home decorating and design, crafts, gardening, or home improvement books, check wherever quality books are sold. Or visit us at: bhgbooks.com.

Cover Photograph:
Doug Heatherington
Pictured on front cover:
Chocolate-Cranberry Cheesecake (recipe, page 78), Sour Cream Sugar Cookies (recipe, page 106) and Chocolate Cookie Cutouts (recipe, page 110).

Better Homes and Gardens®

CHRISTMAS COOKING
FROM THE HEART™

Editor: Winifred Moranville
Contributing Recipe Editor: M. Peg Smith
Contributing Writers: Amber Barz, Richard Swearinger
Recipe Developer: Ellen Boeke
Contributing Art Director/Graphic Designer: Kimberly B. Zarley
Copy Chief: Terri Fredrickson
Publishing Operations Manager: Karen Schirm
Edit and Design Production Coordinator: Mary Lee Gavin
Book Production Managers: Pam Kvitne, Marjorie J. Schenkelberg, Rick von Holdt, Mark Weaver
Contributing Copy Editor: Kim Catanzarite
Contributing Proofreaders: Gretchen Kauffman, Susan J. Kling, Donna Segal
Indexer: Spectrum Communication Services
Editorial Assistants: Cheryl Eckert, Kaye Chabot
Test Kitchen Director: Lynn Blanchard
Test Kitchen Product Supervisor: Jill Moberly

Meredith® Books
Editor in Chief: Linda Raglan Cunningham
Design Director: Matt Strelecki
Managing Editor: Gregory H. Kayko
Executive Editor, Food and Crafts: Jennifer Dorland Darling

Publisher: James D. Blume
Executive Director, Marketing: Jeffrey Myers
Executive Director, New Business Development: Todd M. Davis
Executive Director, Sales: Ken Zagor
Director, Operations: George A. Susral
Director, Production: Douglas M. Johnston
Business Director: Jim Leonard

Vice President and General Manager: Douglas J. Guendel

Better Homes and Gardens® Magazine
Editor in Chief: Karol DeWulf Nickell
Deputy Editor, Home Design: Oma Blaise Ford
Deputy Editor, Food and Entertaining: Nancy Wall Hopkins

Meredith Publishing Group
President, Publishing Group: Stephen M. Lacy
Vice President Publishing Director: Bob Mate

Meredith Corporation
Chairman and Chief Executive Officer: William T. Kerr

In Memoriam: E. T. Meredith III (1933-2003)

Table of Contents

Sour Cream Sugar Cookies
(recipe, page 106) and
Chocolate Cookie Cutouts
(recipe, page 110)

Poires Belle Hélène
(recipe, page 82)

Christmas Cooking from the Heart

celebrates an exciting array of foods and flavors from across America and shows you how to star them on your holiday table. You'll find festive recipes that feature the bounty of our fields, orchards, woodlands, and waters—from Florida's citrus to Seattle's smoked salmon. Recipes also tap into regionally unique food products, such as New England maple syrup, Kentucky bourbon, and fascinating cheeses handcrafted on farmsteads all across the country.

Once upon a time, people from the Great Plains likely had to travel to New England to taste a true Vermont cheddar. At the same time, many New Englanders may have never tasted chorizo until they ventured to the Southwest. And if you were living in the middle of the country, the taste of fresh seafood was likely a distant memory culled from a rare trip or two to the ocean.

There's no doubt about it—now is a great time to be cooking in America. Never has there been a better supply of fresh, high-quality foods available to home cooks everywhere. Thanks to today's far-reaching networks of distributors, foods from across the country can be easily found at well-stocked grocery stores and at discount retailers. If you have trouble locating a particular ingredient, turn to Sources, page 156; also, in most cases you'll find alternative ingredient options for any less-common specialty ingredients in the recipes.

This cookbook features regionally distinct foods that are widely available, with a particular focus on foods in-season during the holidays. You'll love what these foods bring to your holiday cooking.

And when it comes to putting on feasts for Thanksgiving, Christmas, and New Year's, you'll love the clever ways to imbue favorite holiday foods—from turkey and roasted meats to stuffing and sweet potatoes—with distinct regional flavors. Even the ever-popular green bean casserole gets a fresh, new update.

What's to drink? Raise a glass to American wines, because you'll soon be learning how easy it is to perfectly match them with the splendid holiday fare featured in this book.

Cooking from the heart has long been a cherished part of the holiday season. While you're tapping into this time-honored tradition, tap into the wonderful foods available today. No matter which recipes you choose from this book, you can be sure that you're treating family and friends to some of the best foods this country has to offer.

Ol' South Pralines (recipe, page 119)

Farm-Inspired Holiday Feasts

THE MENUS FOR THIS YEAR'S HOLIDAY table would be right at home in farmhouses across America, as they tap into the bounty of our fields, ranches, citrus groves, orchards, and timbers. Start with one of the regionally inspired main dishes: a Maple-Glazed Turkey from New England, a good old Glazed Baked Ham from the South, a hearty pork roast from the Heartland, or a succulent leg of Colorado lamb. Then call on the menu ideas here to bring a regional theme to your holiday, or mix and match the side-dish recipes to create your own cross-country feast.

Apple-Stuffed Pork Loin (recipe, page 13)

Lobster Bisque

Thanks to dedicated fish purveyors across the country, you don't have to live in New England to savor a fine lobster bisque. It's one of the most classic and sumptuous ways to kick off a holiday meal—or any festive dinner party throughout the year.

Start to Finish: 1 hour
Makes: 8 first-course servings

2	8-ounce fresh or frozen lobster tails
1	14-ounce can chicken broth
1	small onion, chopped (½ cup)
½	cup finely chopped carrot
½	cup dry white wine
2	tablespoons curry powder
1	tablespoon tomato paste
1	bay leaf
3	cups half-and-half, light cream, or whipping cream
¼	cup butter, melted
¼	cup all-purpose flour
3	tablespoons cognac
1	tablespoon snipped fresh parsley
	Salt
	Freshly ground black pepper
	Fresh chives

1. Thaw lobster tails, if frozen; rinse under cold running water. In a heavy 3-quart saucepan combine chicken broth, onion, and carrot; bring to boiling. Add lobster tails. Simmer, covered, for 8 to 12 minutes or until shells turn bright red and lobster meat is tender. Remove lobster tails; cool. Strain broth. Return strained broth to saucepan. Stir in wine, curry powder, tomato paste, and bay leaf. Bring to boiling; reduce heat. Simmer, uncovered, for 10 minutes. Meanwhile, remove meat from lobster tails and coarsely chop.

2. Stir half-and-half into broth mixture in saucepan. Stir together melted butter and flour. Stir into cream mixture. Cook and stir until thickened and bubbly; cook for 1 minute more. Stir in lobster meat, cognac, and parsley. Heat through. Discard bay leaf.

3. Season to taste with salt and pepper. Ladle into soup bowls. Garnish with fresh chives.

Crab Soup

A classic cream soup from South Carolina, this superb dish traditionally is called "she-crab soup" and is prepared in the spring with fresh crab roe. During the winter holidays achieve the hallmark rosy blush by substituting paprika for the coral-color roe.

Start to Finish: 30 minutes
Makes: 8 first-course servings

1	pound fresh or frozen cooked lump crab meat, flaked and cartilage removed, or three 6½-ounce cans lump crab meat, drained and flaked
¼	cup butter or margarine
1	cup finely chopped onion (1 large)
½	cup finely chopped celery (1 stalk)
1	shallot, finely chopped
¼	cup all-purpose flour
1	teaspoon finely shredded lemon peel
¾	teaspoon paprika
½	teaspoon salt
½	teaspoon freshly ground black pepper

Lobster Bisque

Few dashes cayenne pepper
4 cups milk
2 cups half-and-half or light cream
1 teaspoon Worcestershire sauce
¼ cup dry sherry

1. Thaw crab meat, if frozen; set aside. In a Dutch oven melt butter over medium heat. Add onion, celery, and shallot; cook about 5 minutes or until vegetables are tender.

2. Add flour, lemon peel, paprika, salt, black pepper, and cayenne pepper to Dutch oven; cook for 1 minute. Gradually stir in milk, half-and-half, and Worcestershire sauce until smooth. Cook and stir until slightly thickened and bubbly. Stir in crab meat and sherry; heat through but do not boil. Season to taste.

Hickory Nut Salad with Apples

You'll be surprised how wonderfully the apples, hickory nuts, fennel, and cider-infused dressing meld in this delightful salad. Boston (or butterhead) lettuce, with its pliant, buttery texture, provides the perfect contrast to the crunchy ingredients.

Start to Finish: 25 minutes
Makes: 8 first-course servings

¼ cup apple cider vinegar
2 cloves garlic, minced
2 teaspoons Dijon-style mustard
½ teaspoon salt
¼ teaspoon ground black pepper
¼ cup canola oil or salad oil
¼ cup walnut oil
1 medium fennel bulb
8 cups torn Boston or Bibb lettuce
2 cups torn curly endive
1 cup coarsely chopped hickory nuts, pecans, or walnuts, toasted (see note, page 131)
2 medium tart red apples, cored and thinly sliced

Hickory Nut Salad with Apples

1. In a small bowl combine vinegar, garlic, mustard, salt, and pepper. Whisk in canola and walnut oils until well blended. Set dressing aside.

2. To prepare fennel, cut off and discard upper stalks. (If desired, reserve fennel fronds for garnish.) Remove any wilted outer layers and cut a thin slice from fennel base. Wash fennel; cut in half lengthwise and remove core. Cut crosswise into thin slices. In a very large bowl, combine sliced fennel, lettuce, endive, nuts, and sliced apples. Add dressing; toss to coat. Transfer to a serving platter.

9

Flavors of the West at Christmas

Smoked Salmon Chowder

Stuffed Leg of Lamb (recipe, page 14)

Parsnip-Potato Puree (recipe, page 21)

Green Beans and Fennel (recipe, page 19)

Purchased sourdough bread

Orchard Pear Tart (recipe, page 82)

Fresh Mushroom Soup

In recent years a wider variety of mushrooms has become available on the market, elevating mushroom soup status from a standard casserole ingredient to a lovely sit-down starter worthy of a holiday meal.

Start to Finish: 45 minutes
Makes: 8 to 10 first-course servings

9 ounces fresh oyster mushrooms
12 ounces fresh shiitake or button mushrooms
½ cup chopped shallots
¼ cup butter
¼ cup all-purpose flour
¾ teaspoon salt
¼ teaspoon coarsely ground black pepper
3 cups vegetable broth or chicken broth
3 cups half-and-half or light cream
¼ teaspoon ground saffron or saffron threads, crushed
Saffron threads (optional)

1. Remove stems from the mushrooms; discard. Coarsely chop the oyster mushrooms and half of the shiitake mushrooms; set aside. Chop the remaining mushrooms.

2. In a 4-quart Dutch oven or large saucepan cook mushrooms and shallots in hot butter over medium-high heat for 4 to 5 minutes or until tender, stirring occasionally. Stir in flour, salt, and pepper. Add broth. Cook and stir over medium heat until slightly thickened and bubbly. Cook and stir 1 minute more. Stir in half-and-half and saffron; heat through.

3. To serve, ladle soup into bowls. If desired, top with saffron threads.

Smoked Salmon Chowder

This recipe takes chowder to another level. Often enjoyed as an appetizer, smoked salmon provides a rich and smoky flavor for this Northwestern-inspired meal. Later in the winter, ladle a whole bowl for a cozy and warming soup supper.

Prep: 15 minutes Cook: 25 minutes
Makes: 6 main-dish or 8 appetizer servings

¼ cup butter
2 cups sliced leeks
1 clove garlic, minced
2 tablespoons all-purpose flour
3 cups fish stock or vegetable stock
1½ pounds yellow potatoes, peeled and cut into ¼-inch cubes (3 cups)
1 teaspoon salt
¾ pound smoked salmon, cut into bite-size pieces
¾ cup whipping cream
Sliced leeks (optional)
Ground black pepper

1. In a 6-quart Dutch oven melt butter over medium heat. Add the 2 cups leeks and garlic; cook and stir for 5 minutes or until soft. Stir in flour; cook and stir for 2 minutes more.

2. Gradually whisk the stock into the leek mixture in Dutch oven until smooth. Add potatoes and salt. Bring to boiling, stirring often. Reduce heat to medium. Simmer, covered, for 10 to 15 minutes or just until potatoes are tender. Stir in salmon and cream. Heat through. If desired, garnish each serving with additional sliced leeks. Sprinkle with pepper.

Smoked Salmon Chowder

Smoked Salmon The fish used to make smoked salmon can come from both Atlantic and Pacific waters, although the Pacific Northwest is particularly famous for its smoked salmon products. For the luscious Smoked Salmon Chowder, choose a salmon that was hot-smoked versus cold-smoked. Hot-smoked salmon is smoked at temperatures that are high enough to cook it through, while cold-smoked salmon is smoked at lower temperatures, imbuing the fish with flavor without cooking it through (lox-style salmon is an example). While packaging labels sometimes fail to say which smoking method was used, it's easy to tell simply by looking at the fish. Cold-smoked salmon is a soft, delicate product that peels away in layers. Hot-smoked salmon is generally deeper in color, harder in texture, and easily broken into chunks. Hot-smoked salmon is also available in cans, while the cold-smoked variety is not. Use hot-smoked salmon in these recipes unless lox-style salmon is specifically called for.

Maple-Glazed Turkey with
Orange-Parsley Stuffing

Maple-Glazed Turkey with Orange-Parsley Stuffing

Who doesn't love maple syrup? When sparked with a little Dijon mustard and enriched with butter and Worcestershire sauce, New England's most famous staple makes an irresistible glaze for your holiday bird. If desired, add kumquats, sage sprigs, and cranberries to garnish the serving platter.

**Prep: 45 minutes Roast: 3¾ hours
Stand: 15 minutes Oven: 325°F
Makes: 12 to 14 servings**

10	cups dry bread cubes
1	cup snipped fresh parsley
½	cup chopped onion
4	teaspoons finely shredded orange peel
1	teaspoon dried marjoram, crushed
1	teaspoon dried thyme, crushed
2	cloves garlic, minced
¼	cup butter, melted
2	slightly beaten eggs
⅓	cup orange juice
½	cup water
1	12- to 14-pound turkey
	Salt and ground black pepper
⅔	cup pure maple syrup
⅓	cup Dijon-style mustard
2	tablespoons butter
4	teaspoons Worcestershire sauce

1. For stuffing, in a large bowl combine bread cubes, parsley, onion, orange peel, marjoram, thyme, garlic, ½ teaspoon *salt*, and ¼ teaspoon *ground black pepper*. Mix well.

2. In a small bowl stir together the ¼ cup melted butter, beaten eggs, orange juice, and water. Pour over and toss with bread mixture. If desired, add additional water to reach desired moistness.

3. Rinse the inside of turkey; pat dry with paper towels. Season body cavity of turkey with salt and pepper. Loosely spoon some of the stuffing into neck cavity. Skewer neck skin to back. Loosely spoon more of the stuffing into body cavity. Tuck drumsticks under tail skin or tie to tail. Twist wing tips under the back. Transfer any remaining stuffing to a baking dish; cover and chill stuffing in the refrigerator.

4. On a rack in a shallow roasting pan place turkey, breast side up. Insert a meat thermometer into the center of one of the inside thigh muscles. The bulb should not touch the bone. Loosely cover turkey with foil.

5. Roast stuffed turkey in a 325° oven for 3¾ to 4½ hours. Remove foil during the last 45 minutes of roasting. Cut band of skin or string between drumsticks to allow thighs to cook evenly.

6. Meanwhile, for maple glaze, in a small saucepan combine maple syrup, mustard, the 2 tablespoons butter, and Worcestershire sauce. Cook and stir over medium heat until butter is melted. During the last 30 minutes of roasting, brush with the maple glaze. Roast until the meat thermometer registers 180°F and the center of the stuffing registers 165°F. (The juices should run clear and drumsticks should move easily in their sockets.)

7. Bake the dish of stuffing, covered, alongside turkey the last 40 to 45 minutes of roasting time. Uncover baking dish the last 15 minutes of roasting time. Remove turkey from oven. Cover and let stand for 15 to 20 minutes before carving.

8. To serve, remove the stuffing from turkey; transfer stuffing to a serving bowl. Carve the turkey; serve stuffing alongside.

Cranberry-Kumquat Relish

This relish was designed with the Maple-Glazed Turkey in mind, but it pairs nicely with just about any poultry you serve during the holidays. An added bonus: The relish becomes a conversation piece as guests try to guess the secret ingredient (it's kumquats, which bring a citruslike sweet-tart flavor).

Prep: 20 minutes
Makes: 2½ cups relish

   2   cups cranberries (½ pound)
   ¾   cup fresh kumquats, seeded and
       coarsely chopped (4 ounces)
   ⅔   cup granulated sugar
   ⅔   cup packed brown sugar
   ½   cup orange juice
   1   teaspoon grated fresh ginger or
       ¼ teaspoon ground ginger
   ¼   cup coarsely chopped walnuts

1. In a medium saucepan combine cranberries, kumquats, granulated sugar, brown sugar, orange juice, and ginger. Bring cranberry mixture to boiling. Reduce heat. Simmer, uncovered, over medium-low heat for 8 minutes, stirring frequently. Stir in walnuts.

Apple-Stuffed Pork Loin

Pork is raised abundantly on farms throughout the Midwest, and it naturally makes a flavorful, succulent meat at holiday tables in the region. Enjoy this special version enhanced with a fruity, spicy stuffing. Serve with mashed potatoes and gravy. Pictured on page 7.

Prep: 30 minutes Roast: 2¼ hours
Stand: 10 minutes Oven: 325°F
Makes: 10 to 12 servings

   2   to 3 stalks celery, coarsely chopped
       (1 to 1½ cups)
   1   cup coarsely chopped onion
   ½   cup butter
   3   cups chopped tart red apples
   ½   teaspoon ground allspice
   ¼   teaspoon ground cardamom
   5   cups dry bread cubes
   ½   cup raisins (optional)
   1   3- to 4-pound boneless double pork loin
       roast (tied)
       Dash salt
       Dash ground black pepper
       Dash garlic powder

1. For stuffing, in a large skillet cook the celery and onion in butter until vegetables are tender but not brown. Stir in chopped apples, allspice, and cardamom. Cook, uncovered, for 5 minutes or until apple is tender, stirring occasionally. Transfer apple mixture to a very large bowl. Add bread cubes and, if desired, the raisins. Toss gently to combine.

2. Untie the roast and separate into halves.* Trim excess fat from the meat. Spoon about 1½ cups of the apple stuffing over half of the meat. Spoon remaining stuffing into a 1½-quart baking dish; cover and chill in refrigerator.

3. Reassemble roast. Tie with string to secure. Place on a rack in a roasting pan. Insert meat thermometer into the center of the thickest portion of the meat. Sprinkle meat with salt, pepper, and garlic powder.

4. Roast pork loin, uncovered, in a 325° oven for 2¼ to 2¾ hours or until a meat thermometer registers 155°F. During the last 45 minutes of roasting time, bake the dish of apple stuffing, uncovered, alongside the roast until heated through. Let the roast stand, covered, for 10 minutes before slicing (the meat temperature will rise 5°F during standing time).

*Note: *If you prefer not to untie and stuff the roast, simply place all the stuffing in a 2-quart casserole dish and bake it, uncovered, alongside the roast during the last 45 to 50 minutes of cooking time or until stuffing is heated through.*

Glazed Baked Ham

3. Meanwhile, for glaze, in a medium saucepan stir together brown sugar, honey, orange juice, bourbon, and mustard. Cook and stir over medium heat until sugar dissolves. Brush about ¼ cup of the glaze over ham. Bake, uncovered, for 20 to 30 minutes more or until meat thermometer registers 135°F. Let ham stand for 15 minutes before carving. (The meat temperature will rise 5° during standing.)

4. Reheat remaining glaze and serve with ham.

Stuffed Leg of Lamb

In America lamb has lagged behind the popularity of other red meats. That's changing, in part because American chefs are featuring it on their menus. While Australian and New Zealand lamb used to dominate the market, many chefs today prefer lamb from Colorado and Washington for its richer texture and fuller flavor.

Prep: 45 minutes Roast: 1¼ hours
Stand: 20 minutes Marinate: 6 hours
Oven: 325°F Makes: 10 servings

```
 1   5- to 6-pound boned leg of lamb*
 ¾   cup dry red wine
 ⅓   cup Worcestershire sauce
 2   6-ounce packages long grain and wild
     rice mix
 2   cups finely chopped onion
 2   6-ounce packages dried apricots,
     chopped
 1   cup water
 ½   cup snipped fresh basil or 2 tablespoons
     dried basil, crushed
 2   teaspoons lemon-pepper seasoning
```

1. Untie roast. Remove fell (paper-thin pinkish red layer), if present, from outer surface of lamb. Trim off fat. Place lamb in very large self-sealing plastic bag set in a 3-quart rectangular baking dish. Stir together red wine and Worcestershire sauce; pour over lamb. Seal bag and marinate in refrigerator for 6 hours or overnight, turning the bag occasionally.

Glazed Baked Ham

Few holiday meats are easier to cook than a ham. This one brings the graciousness and warmth of the South to your table.

Prep: 15 minutes Bake: 1¼ hours, 20 minutes
Stand: 15 minutes Oven: 325°F
Makes: 16 to 20 servings

```
 1   5-to-6 pound cooked ham (rump half or
     shank portion)
     Whole cloves (about 1 teaspoon)
 1   cup packed brown sugar
 ½   cup honey
 ¼   cup orange juice
 ¼   cup bourbon or orange juice
 2   tablespoons Dijon-style mustard
```

1. Score ham by making diagonal cuts in a diamond pattern. To stud the ham with cloves, push in the long end of a clove at diamond intersections. Place ham on a rack in a shallow roasting pan. Insert a meat thermometer, making sure the thermometer does not touch the bone.

2. Bake ham in a 325° oven until meat thermometer registers 125°F. For rump half, allow 1¼ to 1½ hours; for shank, allow 1¾ to 2 hours.

Green Beans and Fennel
(recipe, page 19)

Stuffed Leg of Lamb

2. In a large saucepan prepare rice mix according to package directions, adding chopped onion with the rice and seasoning packet. Meanwhile, in a medium saucepan combine chopped apricots and water. Bring to boiling. Remove from heat, cover, and let stand for 5 minutes.

3. In a large bowl stir together cooked rice mixture, undrained apricot mixture, basil, and lemon-pepper seasoning; mix well and set aside.

4. Remove meat from bag; discard marinade. To butterfly the lamb, make a lengthwise cut down the center of the meat, cutting to but not through the other side. Make 2 parallel cuts on each side of the center cut to flatten the meat. Place meat, boned side up, between 2 sheets of plastic wrap. Pound meat with a meat mallet to an even thickness. Spread 2 cups of the rice mixture over roast. Roll up; tie securely with string.

5. Place roast, seam side down, on a rack in a shallow roasting pan. Insert a meat thermometer into thickest portion of meat. Roast, uncovered, in a 325° oven for 1¼ to 1¾ hours or until a meat thermometer registers 150°F. Let lamb stand for 15 minutes before carving.

6. Meanwhile, place remaining rice mixture in a 2-quart casserole; cover. Bake alongside lamb during the last 30 to 35 minutes of roasting and standing time. Remove the string from meat before serving.

*Note: If your supermarket doesn't regularly stock leg of lamb, order the cut a few days in advance and ask the butcher to bone and butterfly it for you. Use a meat thermometer to determine doneness.

Texas Red Grapefruit Salad

Texas ruby-red grapefruit is a beautiful way to brighten the table during the holidays and is the inspiration for this colorful salad. But you can use any in-season grapefruit for this recipe.

Prep: 30 minutes Chill: 6 hours
Makes: 9 servings

- 4 **cups grapefruit sections**
  (9 to 10 grapefruits)
- 1 **cup sugar**
- 2 **envelopes unflavored gelatin**
- ¾ **cup cold water**
- ½ **cup chopped pecans**
- 1 **or 2 drops red food coloring (optional)**
  Whipped cream
  Grapefruit peel curls

1. In a large bowl combine grapefruit sections and ¾ cup of the sugar; set aside. In a small bowl combine gelatin and ½ cup of the cold water; let stand for 5 minutes.

2. Meanwhile, in a medium saucepan combine the remaining sugar and remaining cold water. Heat and stir until sugar is dissolved. Add gelatin mixture, grapefruit mixture, nuts, and, if desired, food coloring. Cook and stir until sugar is completely dissolved. Pour grapefruit mixture into a 2-quart mold or square baking dish. Cover; chill at least 6 hours. To serve, if using a mold, unmold salad. Serve with whipped cream and grapefruit peel curls.

Texas Red Grapefruit Salad

Red Grapefruit Grapefruit flourishes in Arizona, California, Florida, and Texas, but the Lone Star State is most famous for the beautiful ruby-red variety that stars in Texas Red Grapefruit Salad. In fact, red grapefruit is the official state fruit of Texas. Look for red grapefruit starting in November. Its peak season falls between Christmas and April—just in time for the holidays.

Southern Ambrosia

Popular in the South, ambrosia is a dish of chilled fruit and coconut that's traditionally presented in a pretty glass bowl. While it's often served as a dessert, this side-dish version really brightens up roasted meats.

Prep: 25 minutes Chill: 4 hours
Makes: 6 to 8 servings

- 1 **medium fresh pineapple, peeled, cored,**
  and cut into ½-inch chunks (about
  4½ cups)
- 6 **oranges, peeled, seeded, and cut into**
  ½-inch segments
- 1 **cup flaked frozen coconut, thawed***
- ⅓ **cup sugar**
- 3 **tablespoons dry sherry or orange juice**

1. In a large serving bowl combine the pineapple and oranges. In a small bowl stir together the coconut, sugar, and sherry. Combine with fruit and toss lightly. Cover and chill for at least 4 hours or up to 8 hours.

*Note: *Frozen flaked coconut is widely available in supermarkets in the South. If you can't find this frozen product where you shop, use 1 cup packaged flaked coconut in place of the frozen coconut.*

Creamy Cranberry Salad

At potlucks or church basement suppers in the Midwest, it's generally a sure bet that you'll find a gelatin salad or two. Such salads are lovely ways to show off regional and seasonal fruits, such as the cranberries that spark the salad here.

Prep: 15 minutes Chill: 4 hours
Makes: 6 servings

- ½ **cup water**
- 1 **envelope unflavored gelatin**
- 1 **8-ounce package cream cheese or reduced-fat cream cheese (Neufchâtel), softened**
- 1 **12-ounce package desired flavor cranberry-fruit sauce, such as cranberry-strawberry or cranberry-raspberry**
- ¼ **cup chopped pecans**
  Fresh cranberries, salad greens, and orange peel (optional)

1. In a 1-cup glass measure stir together the water and gelatin; let stand for 5 minutes to soften.

2. Meanwhile, in a medium mixing bowl, beat cream cheese with an electric mixer on low to medium speed until smooth. Beat in cranberry-fruit sauce and pecans; set aside.

3. In a medium saucepan pour in water to depth of 1 inch; place the glass measure with gelatin mixture in the water. Heat until gelatin dissolves, stirring constantly.

4. Stir gelatin mixture into cranberry mixture. Pour into a 3½- or 4-cup mold. Cover and chill in the refrigerator for at least 4 hours or until firm. Unmold onto a serving plate. If desired, garnish with fresh cranberries, salad greens, and twisted orange peel.

Southern Ambrosia

Southern Christmas

Crab Soup (recipe, page 8)

Glazed Baked Ham (recipe, page 14)

Southern Ambrosia

Green Bean and Sweet Onion Gratin (recipe, page 20)

Traditional Corn Bread Dressing (recipe, page 22)

Slow-Cooker Holiday Potatoes (recipe, page 25)

Luscious Orange Sponge Cake (recipe, page 76)

A Heartland Holiday

Fresh Mushroom Soup (recipe, page 10)

Apple-Stuffed Pork Loin (recipe, page 13)

Best-Ever Corn Pudding

Wild Rice Rolls (recipe, page 66)

Mashed potatoes and Pan Gravy (recipe, page 24)

Wisconsin Cheese Pie (recipe, page 78)

Best-Ever Corn Pudding

Sweet corn is a source of bragging rights for Midwesterners—they all think the corn from their own state is best. Believe it or not, such rivalries exist at the county level too! Here is one undisputed champion of a sweet corn lover's favorite dish.

Prep: 20 minutes Bake: 40 minutes
Oven: 325°F Makes: 8 servings

> ¼ cup butter
> 2 tablespoons granulated sugar
> 2 tablespoons all-purpose flour
> ½ cup half-and-half or light cream
> 4 slightly beaten eggs
> 1½ teaspoons baking powder
> 2 15-ounce cans yellow or white whole kernel corn, drained, or one 16-ounce bag frozen whole kernel corn, thawed and drained
> 2 tablespoons packed brown sugar
> 2 tablespoons butter, melted
> ¼ teaspoon ground cinnamon (optional)

1. In a large saucepan cook and stir the ¼ cup butter and granulated sugar over medium heat until the butter is melted. Remove from heat. Stir in flour. Stir in half-and-half, eggs, and baking powder. Stir in corn until combined. Spoon into a buttered 1½-quart casserole.

2. Bake corn mixture, uncovered, in a 325° oven for 35 minutes. Meanwhile, combine the brown sugar, 2 tablespoons melted butter, and (if desired) cinnamon. Spoon over the corn mixture. Bake for 5 minutes more or until a knife inserted near the center comes out clean.

Best-Ever Corn Pudding

Cheesy Wild Rice Casserole

Minnesotans will tell you that wild rice—which grows in the marshes of the Great Lakes—is actually a member of the grass family and isn't rice at all. Somehow, Cheesy Marsh Grass Casserole just doesn't sound appetizing, so go ahead and call it wild rice and enjoy it in this creamy casserole that goes great with ham, beef, or poultry.

Prep: 20 minutes Bake: 35 minutes
Stand: 5 minutes Oven: 375°F
Makes: 6 to 8 servings

- 1 6-ounce package long grain and wild rice mix
- 1 4-ounce can (drained weight) sliced mushrooms, drained
- 2½ cups water
- 1 10-ounce package frozen chopped spinach
- ¾ cup chopped onion
- 1 tablespoon butter or margarine
- 2 teaspoons prepared mustard
- ¼ teaspoon ground nutmeg
- 1 8-ounce package cream cheese, cut into cubes

1. In a 2-quart casserole combine rice mix and seasoning packet with mushrooms. In a medium saucepan combine water, spinach, onion, butter, mustard, and nutmeg. Bring to boiling; remove from heat. Stir spinach mixture; pour over rice mixture. Stir in cream cheese.

2. Bake, covered, in a 375° oven 20 minutes. Stir rice mixture. Cover; bake 15 to 20 minutes more or until rice is tender. Stir again. Let stand for 5 minutes before serving.

Make-Ahead Tip: *Assemble the casserole; refrigerate up to 2 hours before baking. Add a few minutes to the baking time to heat the casserole through.*

Green Beans and Fennel

Looking a little like a potbellied cousin to celery, fennel imparts a licorice flavor and delightful crunch. Hint: To crush fennel seeds, place them on a cutting board and roll over them with a rolling pin. Pictured on page 15.

Start to Finish: 30 minutes
Makes: 8 to 10 servings

- 2 tablespoons butter, softened
- 1½ teaspoons fennel seeds, crushed
- 1½ teaspoons finely shredded lemon peel
- ¾ teaspoon coarsely ground black pepper
- ¼ teaspoon salt
- 3 fennel bulbs (3 pounds)
- 1¾ pounds fresh green beans, trimmed if desired

1. In a large bowl stir together butter, fennel seeds, lemon peel, pepper, and salt; set aside.

2. Cut off and discard upper stalks of fennel bulbs. Remove any wilted outer layers; cut off a thin slice from the fennel base. Wash fennel; cut into quarters. Remove cores. Cut fennel lengthwise into ¼-inch strips.

3. In a 4-quart Dutch oven place beans. Cook beans, covered, in a small amount of boiling salted water for 4 to 5 minutes. Add fennel strips to beans. Cook for 6 to 10 minutes more or until vegetables are crisp-tender. Drain.

4. Add fennel and beans to the bowl with the seasoned butter. Toss until vegetables are coated. Transfer to a serving dish.

Green Bean and Sweet Onion Gratin

This gourmet take on the ever-popular green bean casserole calls on delicious sweet onions.

Prep: 30 minutes Bake: 35 minutes
Stand: 10 minutes Oven: 325°F
Makes: 8 to 10 servings

- **2 16-ounce packages frozen cut green beans**
- **1½ pounds sweet onions, halved and thinly sliced**
- **⅓ cup butter or margarine**
- **⅓ cup all-purpose flour**
- **¼ teaspoon ground black pepper**
- **⅛ teaspoon ground nutmeg**
- **1 14-ounce can chicken broth**
- **1½ cups half-and-half, light cream, or milk**
- **2¼ cups soft bread crumbs (4 to 5 slices)**
- **⅓ cup grated Parmesan cheese**
- **3 tablespoons olive oil**

1. Cook frozen green beans according to package directions; drain well and set aside.

2. Meanwhile, in a large saucepan or 4-quart Dutch oven cook onion slices in a small amount of boiling water for 4 to 5 minutes or until tender. Drain; set aside.

3. In the same saucepan or Dutch oven melt butter. Stir in flour, 1 teaspoon *salt*, the pepper, and nutmeg. Add broth and half-and-half; cook and stir until mixture is thickened and bubbly.

4. In an ungreased 3-quart rectangular baking dish layer half the beans, all the onions, and the remaining beans. Spoon sauce over all.

5. Toss together bread crumbs, cheese, and oil; sprinkle over vegetables. Bake, uncovered, in a 325° oven for 35 to 40 minutes or until bubbly. Let stand for 10 minutes before serving.

Make-Ahead Tip: *Prepare gratin as directed, except do not top with the bread crumb mixture. Cover baking dish; chill up to 24 hours. Wrap bread crumb mixture separately; chill. To serve, sprinkle bread crumb mixture on vegetables. Bake, uncovered, in a 325° oven for 50 to 55 minutes or until heated through.*

Sweet onions are prized for their sweet, mellow flavor. How can you tell a sweet onion from a regular onion? Most growers put a sticker on sweet onions to identify the variety; many are named for the locales in which they are grown, such as Vidalia, Walla Walla, and Texas 1015. Other varieties include Sweet Imperial and AmeriSweet. Any sweet onion will do for the Green Bean and Sweet Onion Gratin. The Maui Onion and South America's OSO Sweet onions are both in season during the holidays.

Green Bean and Sweet Onion Gratin

Heavenly Potatoes

Rich dairy products and crisp-cooked bacon are the secrets to the heavenly results.

Prep: 40 minutes Bake: 35 minutes
Oven: 325°F Makes: 10 to 12 servings

- 3½ pounds potatoes, peeled and quartered (about 3 cups)
- 1 8-ounce package cream cheese, cut up and softened
- 1 8-ounce carton dairy sour cream
- 2 teaspoons yellow mustard (optional)
- 8 slices bacon, crisp cooked, drained, and crumbled
   Paprika

1. In a Dutch oven or large pan cook potatoes in a moderate amount of boiling water for 20 to 25 minutes or until tender. Drain and mash. Add cream cheese, stirring until combined. Fold in sour cream, mustard (if desired), ¾ teaspoon *salt*, and ½ teaspoon *ground black pepper*. Fold in most of the crumbled bacon (reserve some for garnish).

2. Lightly grease a 2-quart casserole or 2-quart square baking dish; spoon potato mixture into the prepared dish. Sprinkle with paprika. Bake, covered, in a 325° oven for 25 minutes. Uncover; bake for 10 to 15 minutes more or until heated through. Garnish with reserved bacon.

Make-Ahead Tip: *Prepare as directed. Cover unbaked casserole; wrap reserved bacon in plastic wrap. Chill separately in refrigerator up to 24 hours. Bake the casserole, covered, in a 325° oven for 45 minutes. Uncover; bake 10 to 15 minutes more or until heated through. Sprinkle with reserved bacon.*

Potato-Parsnip Puree

An inspired version of mashed potatoes.

Prep: 20 minutes Cook: 30 minutes
Makes: 8 servings

- 1 package (0.5-ounce) dried porcini mushrooms, rinsed well
- ½ cup boiling water

New England Christmas

Lobster Bisque (recipe, page 8)

Maple-Glazed Turkey with Orange-Parsley Stuffing (recipe, page 12)

Hickory Nut Salad with Apples (recipe, page 9)

Heavenly Potatoes

Boston Cream Pie (recipe, page 72)

- 2 pounds parsnips, peeled and sliced
- 1 14-ounce can chicken broth
- 1¾ cups water
- 2 pounds Yukon gold potatoes, peeled and cut into 1½-inch chunks
- 6 tablespoons butter or margarine
- 1 pound leeks, trimmed, white part only, rinsed well and chopped

1. In a small bowl combine dried porcini and the ½ cup boiling water; let stand for 15 minutes. Drain and finely chop porcini; set aside.

2. Meanwhile, in a 4-quart Dutch oven combine parsnips, broth, and the 1¾ cups water. Bring to boiling. Reduce heat; simmer, covered, for 5 minutes. Add potatoes. Return to boiling; reduce heat. Simmer, covered, for 20 minutes or until vegetables are tender. Drain vegetables in a colander set over a large bowl. Reserve ⅓ cup of the broth mixture.

3. In the same Dutch oven melt 2 tablespoons of the butter. Add leeks; cook over medium heat for 5 to 7 minutes or until leeks just start to brown. Add porcini and ½ teaspoon *salt*. Cover and cook for 3 minutes more or until tender.

4. Return potato mixture to Dutch oven; add remaining butter. Mash with a potato masher. Add enough of the reserved broth to reach desired consistency. If necessary, heat through.

Make-Ahead Tip: *Cover and chill in a microwave-safe bowl. Reheat on 100% power (high) for 8 to 10 minutes or until heated through, stirring twice.*

Traditional Corn Bread Dressing

Corn bread dressing is a popular item on Southern holiday tables. Baking powder biscuits make it even better.

Prep: 30 minutes Bake: 45 minutes
Oven: 325°F Makes: 10 to 12 servings

    4 cups crumbled corn bread, dried*
    2 cups crumbled baking powder biscuits,
       dried*
    1 large onion, chopped
    1 cup chopped celery (2 stalks)
   ¼ cup butter or margarine
   1¾ to 2 cups chicken broth
    1 beaten egg
    1 teaspoon dried thyme, crushed
   ½ teaspoon dried sage, crushed

1. In a large bowl combine crumbled corn bread and biscuits; set aside.

2. In a medium saucepan cook onion and celery in butter about 5 minutes or until tender. Remove from heat. Stir in about 1 cup of the broth. Add beaten egg, thyme, and sage. Add onion mixture to corn bread mixture, tossing gently to coat. Add more broth to moisten the stuffing as desired.

3. Transfer stuffing to a 1½-quart shallow baking dish. (Or stuff a 10- to 12-pound turkey.) Bake the stuffing, covered, in a 325° oven about 45 minutes or until heated through (165°F). (When roasted in a turkey, stuffing must reach a temperature of 165°F.)

*Note: *You will need about half an 8-inch square pan of corn bread and three to four (3-inch) biscuits. Crumble and measure 4 cups corn bread and 2 cups biscuits; place crumbled bread in a large roasting pan. To dry, cover loosely with a clean dish towel and let stand for several hours or overnight.*

Corn Bread Dressing with Sausage: Prepare dressing as directed except brown ½ pound bulk pork sausage in a medium skillet; drain. Add to the bread mixture along with the egg.

The Ultimate Scalloped Potatoes

To pull off rich, creamy scalloped potatoes you need two things: the right recipe (this is it!) and the right potato (russets). Russets have high starch content that helps thicken the scalloped potatoes properly. Serve this impressive dish with roasted meats any time throughout the year.

Prep: 30 minutes Bake: 1 hour
Stand: 10 minutes Oven: 350°F
Makes: 6 to 8 servings

    1 cup whipping cream
   ⅓ cup milk
    1 large clove garlic, peeled and crushed
    1 teaspoon salt
   ⅛ teaspoon ground black pepper
    2 pounds russet potatoes, peeled and
       sliced ⅛ inch thick
    1 cup coarsely shredded Gruyère cheese
   ¼ cup finely shredded Parmesan cheese

1. In a small saucepan heat cream, milk, garlic, salt, and pepper over medium-high heat until bubbles appear around edge of pan; remove from heat and let stand for 10 minutes.

2. Place half the sliced potatoes, overlapping slices, in a greased 2-quart baking dish. Pour over half the cream mixture and spread half of the cheeses. Repeat layers. Bake, uncovered, in a 350° oven for 60 to 70 minutes or until top is darkly browned and potatoes are tender.

Praline-Yam
Casserole

Yams versus Sweet Potatoes If you can't tell a yam from a sweet potato, don't worry. You can use both vegetables interchangeably in most recipes, including Praline-Yam Casserole. True yams, grown in tropical climates, have a brownish skin and yellow to white starchy flesh; they're rarely grown or imported into the United States. In fact yams that you see at the supermarket aren't technically true yams—they're a variety of sweet potato. But don't dwell on it—the moist-texture, orange-flesh tuber tastes great in recipes no matter what you call it.

Praline-Yam Casserole

This recipe crosses yams— a favorite Southern tuber—with the flavors of pralines, a favorite New Orleans candy. The result is a sweet and rich bring-a-dish favorite that's perfect for holiday gatherings—a spoonful goes a long way.

Prep: 30 minutes Bake: 35 minutes
Cook: 25 minutes Oven: 350°F
Makes: 8 servings

6	medium yams or sweet potatoes (2 pounds)
1/3	cup milk
1/4	cup packed brown sugar
2	tablespoons butter or margarine, melted
1	egg
1	teaspoon vanilla
1/2	teaspoon salt
3	tablespoons butter or margarine
1/3	cup packed brown sugar
3	tablespoons all-purpose flour
1/3	cup coarsely chopped pecans

1. Scrub yams; cut off woody portions and ends.

2. In a 4-quart Dutch oven cook yams, covered, in enough salted boiling water to cover for 25 to 30 minutes or until tender. Drain and cool slightly. Peel and cut up potatoes.

3. In a large mixing bowl mash yams with a potato masher or an electric mixer on low speed. Add milk, the 1/4 cup brown sugar, the 2 tablespoons melted butter, egg, vanilla, and salt. Beat until fluffy. If desired, add additional milk. Turn into a greased 1 1/2-quart baking dish.

4. In a small saucepan melt the 3 tablespoons butter over low heat. Stir in the 1/3 cup brown sugar, flour, and pecans. Mix well. Spoon pecan mixture over potato mixture. Bake casserole, uncovered, in a 350° oven for 35 minutes or until heated through.

Slow-Cooker Holidays

Put your slow cooker on duty during the holidays; these convenient appliances can make your life easier in the following ways:

• **Save stove top and oven space:** Calling on the slow cooked side dishes in this chapter will help you get a jump-start on prep and free up space where you need it most for your holiday meal.

• **Keep beverages hot:** When entertaining you can keep warm beverages simmering in your cooker on the low-heat setting throughout the party.

• **Toting foods:** When it's your turn to bring a dish, the host will appreciate it when you arrive with one that doesn't need to be reheated (and therefore doesn't take up valuable space in the oven and stove top). To tote foods, after the food is completely cooked, wrap the cooker in heavy foil or several layers of newspaper. Place the cooker in an insulated container. The food should stay hot for up to 2 hours (do not hold longer than 2 hours). Once at the party, plug in the cooker; the food will stay warm on the low-heat setting for a few more hours.

• **Do some of the work the night before:** Cut up or chop all of the vegetables and the meat. Combine the seasonings and the liquids. (Do not precook meats unless they are to be fully cooked before adding to the cooker.) Place vegetables, meat, and seasonings in separate containers; cover and refrigerate. The next day, place the ingredients in the order specified in the recipe into the cooker. Cover; cook as directed.

Pan Gravy

For some families, it's just not a holiday meal without gravy! Here's a basic gravy for poultry; to make gravy for other roasted meats, follow these steps, substituting meat drippings and beef broth for the poultry drippings and chicken broth.

Start to Finish: 15 minutes
Makes: 2 cups (8 to 10 servings)

> Pan drippings from roasted poultry*
> ¼ cup all-purpose flour
> Chicken broth
> Salt and ground black pepper

1. After roasting, transfer the roasted poultry to a serving platter. Pour the pan drippings into a large measuring cup. Scrape the browned bits from the pan into the cup. Skim and reserve fat from the drippings.

2. Pour ¼ cup of the fat* into a medium saucepan (discard remaining fat). Stir in flour. Add enough broth to remaining drippings in the measuring cup to equal 2 cups; add broth mixture all at once to flour mixture in saucepan. Cook and stir over medium heat until thickened and bubbly. Cook and stir for 1 minute more. Season to taste with salt and pepper.

***Note:** If there is no fat, use ¼ cup melted butter.*

Slow-Cooker Creamy Wild Rice Pilaf

News flash: Wild rice—which generally requires a long simmering time on the stove—cooks beautifully in the slow cooker without the precooking step. This creamy side dish tastes great with all holiday meats.

Prep: 25 minutes Cook: 7 hours on low;
3½ hours on high Makes: 12 servings

> 1 cup wild rice, rinsed and drained
> 1 cup regular brown rice
> 1 cup shredded carrots (2 medium)
> 1 cup sliced fresh mushrooms
> ½ cup thinly sliced celery (1 stalk)
> ⅓ cup chopped onion (1 small)

¼ **cup snipped dried apricots**
1 **10¾-ounce can condensed cream of mushroom with roasted garlic or golden mushroom soup**
1 **teaspoon dried thyme, crushed**
1 **teaspoon poultry seasoning**
¾ **teaspoon salt**
½ **teaspoon ground black pepper**
5½ **cups water**
½ **cup dairy sour cream**

1. In a 3½- or 4-quart slow cooker combine uncooked wild rice, uncooked brown rice, carrots, mushrooms, celery, onion, dried apricots, soup, thyme, poultry seasoning, salt, and pepper. Stir in the water.

2. Cover; cook on low-heat setting for 7 to 8 hours or on high-heat setting for 3½ to 4 hours. Stir in sour cream.

Slow-Cooker Holiday Potatoes

You'll love this recipe for three good reasons. First, it calls for Yukon potatoes—rich, gold-fleshed potatoes. Second, it's cooked in a slow cooker (always convenient). And third, it's plenty saucy, so you won't need to make gravy to go with it.

Prep: 25 minutes Cook: 6 hours on low; 3 hours on high Makes: 10 servings

Nonstick cooking spray
1½ **pounds Yukon gold potatoes**
1½ **pounds sweet potatoes**
1 **7-ounce round smoked Gouda cheese or 8 ounces American cheese, shredded**
1 **10¾-ounce can condensed cream of celery soup**
1 **8-ounce carton dairy sour cream**
½ **cup chicken broth**
1 **large onion, sliced**

1. Lightly coat a 4½- or 5-quart slow cooker with cooking spray; set aside.

2. Thinly slice the Yukon gold potatoes (do not peel). Peel and cut sweet potatoes into ¼-inch slices. Set aside.

3. In a medium bowl combine cheese, celery soup, sour cream, and chicken broth. In prepared cooker layer half of the potatoes and half of the onion. Spread half of the soup mixture over mixture in cooker. Repeat layers.

4. Cover; cook on low-heat setting for 6 to 8 hours or on high-heat setting for 3 to 4 hours.

Slow-Cooker Maple-Orange Sweet Potatoes and Carrots

Sweet potatoes may be from the South, but here they take on a little Yankee flair with maple syrup. You'll appreciate the way the slow cooker saves oven and stove top space.

Prep: 20 minutes Cook: 8 hours on low; 4 hours on high Makes: 10 servings

Nonstick cooking spray
1 **16-ounce package peeled baby carrots**
2 **pounds sweet potatoes, peeled and cut into 1½-inch pieces**
1 **cup snipped dried apricots**
½ **cup pure maple syrup or maple-flavored syrup**
¼ **cup frozen orange juice concentrate, thawed**
¼ **cup water**
2 **tablespoons butter or margarine, melted**
½ **teaspoon salt**
¼ **teaspoon ground white pepper**
¼ **teaspoon ground cinnamon**

1. Lightly coat a 3½- or 4-quart slow cooker with cooking spray. In the cooker layer carrots, sweet potatoes, and dried apricots.

2. In a small bowl combine maple syrup, orange juice concentrate, water, melted butter, salt, white pepper, and cinnamon. Pour over mixture in cooker.

3. Cover; cook on low-heat setting for 8 to 9 hours or on high-heat setting for 4 to 4½ hours. Use a slotted spoon to serve.

Appetizers
Across
America

THIS IS NO ORDINARY APPETIZER spread! Tennessee whiskey infuses the meatballs with unmistakable spirit, smoked fish from the Great Lakes makes the dip really come alive, and California dates work their own sweet magic on the puff pastry bites. Those are just three of the many ways in which regional foods and flavors play into the fun starters on these pages. Come along and treat family and friends to a state-by-state sweep of fascinating party foods that will put your guests in an uplifting, glass-raising, anything but bah-humbugging holiday mood.

Smoked Salmon Mousse (recipe, page 34)

Cranberry Wassail

"Wassail" is derived from an old Norse word that translated means "be in good health." Here the old-world brew gets a lively American update with cranberries. Our taste panel found that it's equally good without the brandy.

Prep: 20 minutes Cook: 10 minutes
Makes: 12 to 14 (4-ounce) servings

  1   750-milliliter bottle dry red wine (such as Burgundy)
  2   cups cranberry juice
  1   cup sugar
  ½   cup water
  ¼   cup lemon juice
  6   inches stick cinnamon
  ¼   cup brandy (optional)
       Lemon slices

1. In a large saucepan combine red wine, cranberry juice, sugar, water, lemon juice, and stick cinnamon. Heat and stir until sugar dissolves; continue heating just until bubbly around the edges. Reduce heat. Simmer, uncovered, for 10 minutes. Remove cinnamon with a slotted spoon. Stir in brandy, if desired. Carefully pour punch into a heatproof punch bowl. Garnish with lemon slices. Ladle into heatproof cups.

Southern Peach Punch

One way to make sure your party will be a hit is to kick it off with something exciting to drink. This feisty punch sets a festive tone. Show it off in a clear glass punch bowl to add sparkle to the setting.

Prep: 10 minutes Chill: 4 hours
Makes: 18 (6-ounce) servings

  1   quart orange juice
  3   cups bourbon
  2   cups peach schnapps
  ½   cup grenadine
  1   quart grapefruit carbonated beverage
       Ice Ring (optional)

1. In a punch bowl, combine orange juice, bourbon, peach schnapps, and grenadine. Chill for 4 hours or until thoroughly chilled. Just before serving, add grapefruit carbonated beverage. Ladle into glasses filled with ice.

Ice Ring: *Place grapefruit carbonated beverage that has been allowed to go flat, maraschino cherries, and frozen peach slices into a fluted tube pan; freeze until solid. To unmold, place the bottom of the fluted tube pan in a bowl of warm water for several seconds to loosen the ring, if necessary. Float ring in the punch bowl. If desired garnish with fresh mint sprigs.*

Hot Buttered Rum

This is the kind of warmer-upper you might enjoy at a Colorado lodge after a day on the slopes. No mountains in sight? It's just as heartening after sledding, ice skating, or shoveling snow.

Prep: 5 minutes Cook: 20 minutes
Makes: 8 (8-ounce) servings

  2   quarts apple or pineapple juice
  2   tablespoons packed brown sugar
  3   inches stick cinnamon
  1   teaspoon whole allspice
  1   teaspoon whole cloves
  ¼   teaspoon salt
       Dash ground nutmeg
  1   cup rum
  ¼   cup cold butter, sliced into 8 pats

1. In a large saucepan combine the juice, brown sugar, cinnamon, allspice, cloves, salt, and nutmeg. Bring to boiling; reduce heat. Simmer, covered, for 20 minutes. Stir in rum; return just to boiling. Remove from heat; pour through a strainer to remove whole spices. Place a pat of butter in each of 8 mugs. Pour the hot rum mixture into the mugs.

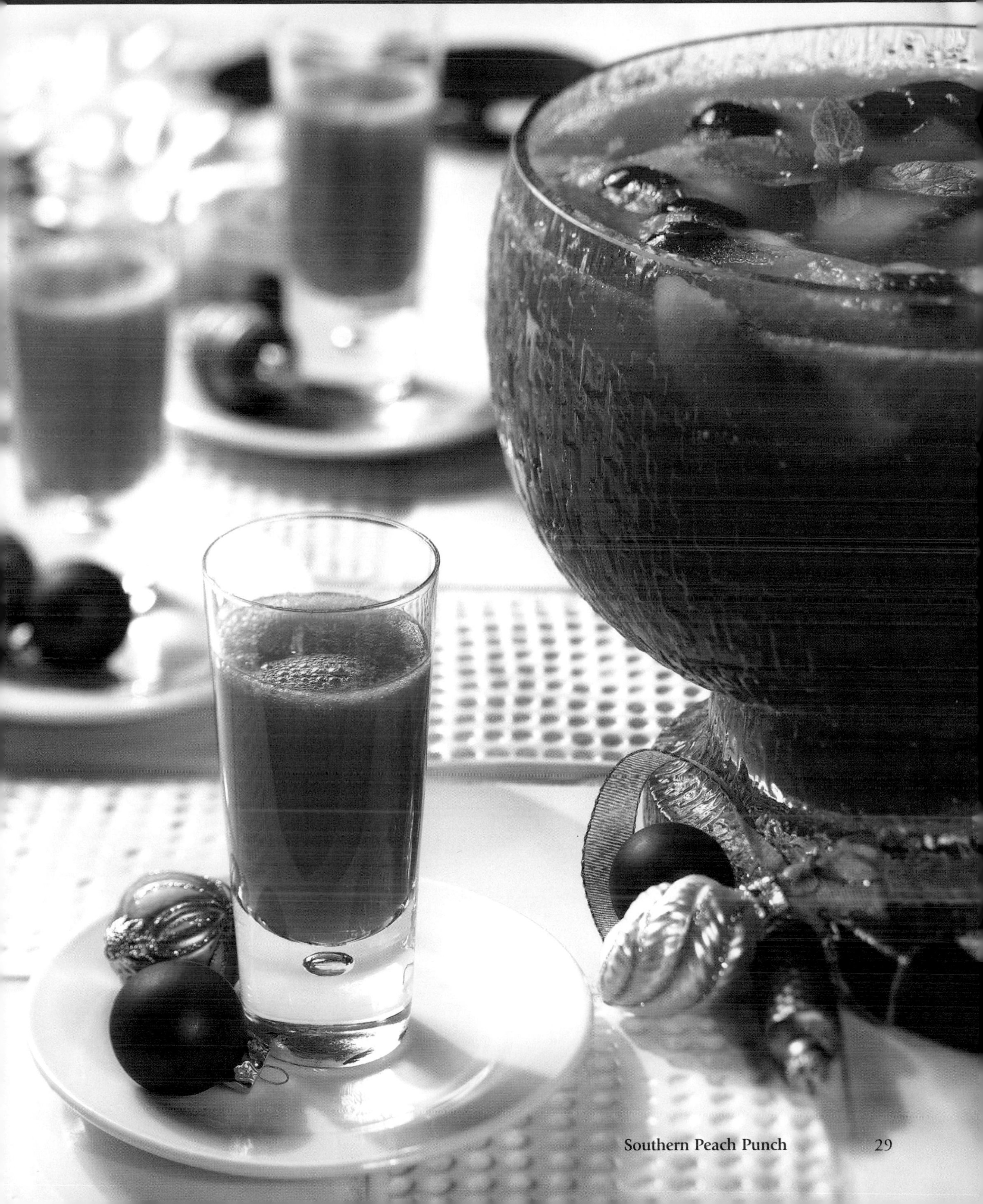

Southern Peach Punch

Buffalo Wings The now-famous Anchor Bar in Buffalo, New York, takes credit for inventing the ever-popular Buffalo Wing. Legend has it that in 1964, a crowd of hungry late-night revelers came into the bar asking for something to eat. Back in the kitchen, the bartender's mother fixed a plate of these tasty tidbits, using chicken wings that she was saving to make stock. The rest is history, and thanks to this all-time favorite all-American appetizer, the humble wing has soared to great heights in popularity. Many popular versions of the appetizers have emerged over the years and are limited only by the imagination of the cook. Some versions, such as Bourbon-Molasses Glazed Chicken Wings, are inspired by regional ingredients.

Bourbon-Molasses Glazed Chicken Wings and Country Ham Gougère (recipe, page 40)

Bourbon-Molasses Glazed Chicken Wings

Distilled from fermented grain, bourbon gets its name from Bourbon County, Kentucky. The spirit adds a deep undertone to these kicky wings.

Prep: 30 minutes Marinate: 1 hour
Bake: 50 minutes Oven: 375°F
Makes: 32 pieces

2 **pounds chicken wings**
3 **tablespoons cider vinegar**
3 **tablespoons molasses**
2 **tablespoons Asian chili sauce**
½ **cup Dijon-style mustard**
½ **cup maple syrup**
2 **tablespoons bourbon**
2 **teaspoons soy sauce**
Nonstick cooking spray
Kosher salt and ground black pepper

1. Remove wing tips from wings and discard or save for making stock. Separate each wing into 2 pieces at the joint.

2. In a bowl combine vinegar, molasses, chili sauce, mustard, maple syrup, bourbon, and soy sauce. Add wings to vinegar mixture in bowl; toss to coat. Cover; marinate in the refrigerator for 1 hour. Line a shallow roasting pan with foil; lightly coat with cooking spray. Drain wings, reserving marinade. Arrange wings in a single layer in prepared pan; sprinkle with salt and pepper. Bake in a 375° oven for 30 minutes, spooning marinade over wings twice. Turn wings over; spoon on additional marinade. Bake for 20 minutes more, spooning on more marinade after 10 minutes. Discard any remaining marinade. Serve warm.

Make-Ahead Tip: *Add wings to marinade as directed; refrigerate up to 4 hours; bake as directed.*

Mandarin Apricot Chicken Wings

Here's an Asian-inspired take on the ever-popular appetizer wing. Rather than explode with heat as the hot-sauced original Buffalo wings do, these drumettes explode with intriguing Asian flavors. Hint: Line the roasting pan with foil for the easiest cleanup possible.

Prep: 15 minutes Bake: 25 minutes
Oven: 400°F Makes: 24 pieces

- 2   pounds chicken wing drumettes (about 24)*
- ⅔   cup bottled sweet-and-sour sauce
- ½   cup snipped dried apricots
- ⅓   cup hoisin sauce
- ¼   cup soy sauce
- 2   tablespoons honey
- 2   cloves garlic, minced
- ¼   teaspoon ground ginger
- ¼   teaspoon five-spice powder
- 1   tablespoon sesame seeds, toasted (see note, page 131)

1. Arrange drumettes in a single layer in a foil-lined baking pan or roasting pan. Bake in a 400° oven for 20 minutes.

2. Meanwhile, in a small saucepan stir together the sweet-and-sour sauce, apricots, hoisin sauce, soy sauce, honey, garlic, ginger, and five-spice powder. Bring to boiling; reduce heat. Simmer, uncovered, for 5 minutes. Remove from heat.

3. Brush about ¼ cup of the sauce mixture over drumettes. Sprinkle with sesame seeds. Bake about 5 minutes more or until the drumettes are no longer pink in the center. Serve drumettes with remaining sauce.

*Note: *If you can't find drumettes, use 12 chicken wings. Cut off and discard wing tips or reserve for making broth. Cut each wing into 2 sections to make drumettes.*

Thai Chicken Wings with Peanut Sauce

Cooks along the West Coast were among the first to bring Southeast Asian flavors to American dining. Here a taste of Thailand imbues popular Buffalo wings.

Prep: 25 minutes Cook: 5 hours on low;
2½ hours on high Makes: 24 pieces

- 2   pounds chicken wing drumettes (about 24) (see note, below left)
- ½   cup bottled salsa
- 2   tablespoons creamy peanut butter
- 1   tablespoon lime juice
- 2   teaspoons soy sauce
- 2   teaspoons grated fresh ginger
- ¼   cup sugar
- ¼   cup creamy peanut butter
- 3   tablespoons soy sauce
- 3   tablespoons water
- 2   cloves garlic, minced

1. Place drumettes in a 3½- or 4-quart slow cooker. Combine salsa, the 2 tablespoons peanut butter, lime juice, the 2 teaspoons soy sauce, and ginger. Pour over drumettes. Toss to coat.

2. Cover and cook on low-heat setting for 5 to 6 hours or on high-heat setting for 2½ to 3 hours.

3. Meanwhile, for the peanut sauce, in a small saucepan use a whisk to combine the sugar, the ¼ cup peanut butter, the 3 tablespoons soy sauce, water, and garlic. Cook over medium-low heat until sugar is dissolved and mixture is smooth; set aside (mixture will thicken as it cools).

4. Drain drumettes; discard cooking liquid. Return drumettes to slow cooker. Gently stir in peanut sauce. Keep drumettes warm in a covered cooker on low-heat setting for up to 2 hours.

Mapled Brie and Apples

The "Brie bake" rises to any special occasion when enhanced with maple syrup and spiked with spirits for extra depth of flavor.

Prep: 20 minutes Bake: 15 minutes
Oven: 425°F/350°F Makes: 20 servings

> Cinnamon Crostini
> 1   8-ounce round Brie cheese
> 3   tablespoons packed brown sugar
> 3   tablespoons maple syrup
> ¼   cup chopped walnuts, toasted (see note, page 131)
> 2   apples, cored and thinly sliced

1. Prepare Cinnamon Crostini. Reduce oven to 350°. Place Brie on an ovenproof platter; bake about 15 minutes or until warm and soft but not runny. (Or place on a microwave-safe platter and microwave on 100-percent power about 40 seconds.)

2. Meanwhile, in a small saucepan stir together brown sugar and maple syrup. Bring to boiling, stirring to dissolve sugar. Reduce heat; simmer, uncovered, about 5 minutes or until slightly thickened. Stir in walnuts. Pour over softened Brie. Serve immediately with Cinnamon Crostini and apple slices.

Cinnamon Crostini: *Cut twenty ½-inch diagonal slices from an 8-ounce French bread baguette. Brush 1 side of slices with 3 tablespoons melted butter. Sprinkle with cinnamon sugar or maple sugar. Arrange on an ungreased baking sheet. Bake in a 425° oven for 6 to 8 minutes or until crisp and light brown.*

Make-Ahead Tip: *Make Cinnamon Crostini the day before and store in a covered container.*

Fruited Brie Bake

Once you've experienced the wonder of melted Brie, it becomes obvious why the Brie bake, described below, has popped up in restaurants everywhere. Bring home the treat with this cranberry-nut-topped version.

Prep: 5 minutes Bake: 10 minutes Oven: 350°F
Makes: 16 to 18 servings

> 2   8-ounce rounds Brie or Camembert cheese
> ½   cup whole cranberry sauce
> ¼   cup apricot preserves
> 2   tablespoons sliced almonds, toasted (see note, page 131)
>   Assorted crackers or toasted baguette slices

1. Cut cheese rounds in half horizontally. Place 2 of the halves, cut sides up, in a shallow baking dish or on an ovenproof serving platter. Spoon the cranberry sauce over each half. Top with remaining cheese halves, cut sides down.

2. Snip any large apricot pieces in preserves. Spoon preserves over cheese rounds; sprinkle with sliced almonds. Bake, uncovered, in a 350° oven for 10 to 12 minutes or until cheese is softened. If desired, transfer to a serving platter. Serve with assorted crackers.

Baked Brie Hailing from the northeast region of France, Brie is one of the world's most beloved cheeses. The buttery, creamy cheese is closely related to Camembert, which comes from the northwest of France; in fact, few cheese experts can tell the difference between the two. These days the "Brie bake"—any recipe that calls for a round of Brie and tops it with a flavorful sweet or savory spread, then warms it in the oven—has become a favorite American party appetizer. Brie bake recipes are a great way to team this world-class cheese with American flavors, as the two recipes on this page demonstrate.

Mapled Brie and Apples

Using Leftover Smoked Salmon If you happen to have some smoked salmon left over from the showstopping Smoked Salmon Mousse at right, consider yourself in luck and use it to make Smoked Salmon Chowder, page 10. Another way to enjoy smoked salmon is in a classic presentation: served on a tray with little bowls of sour cream, lemon wedges, capers, chopped red onions, and crackers. Invite guests to start with a piece of salmon on a cracker, top it with the surrounding ingredients, and finish with a squirt of lemon juice. It's one of the simplest—yet most delightful—ways to enjoy the delicacy.

Smoked Fish Spread

Drive around the Great Lakes region, and you'll see shops selling local brands of smoked fish. Fortunately, the delicacy is available in some supermarkets outside that region. Here's how to transform it into a festive party spread. Hint: If you can't find smoked whitefish, substitute smoked trout or haddock.

Prep: 10 minutes Chill: 4 to 24 hours
Makes: about 1 cup

    6 ounces smoked skinless, boneless
       whitefish
    2 tablespoons mayonnaise or salad
       dressing
  $\frac{1}{2}$ of an 8-ounce package cream cheese,
       softened
    2 tablespoons Dijon-style mustard
  $\frac{1}{4}$ teaspoon ground white pepper

1. Using a fork, finely flake the fish. (Or place fish in a food processor bowl. Cover and process with several on/off turns until fish is finely chopped.) Set aside. In a medium bowl, gradually stir mayonnaise into the softened cream cheese. Stir in the mustard and white pepper. Fold in the fish.

2. Cover and chill in the refrigerator for at least 4 hours or up to 24 hours. To serve, spread fish mixture on crackers.

Smoked Salmon Mousse

Salmon mousse is always an impressive appetizer, but when you use smoked salmon instead of the regular canned salmon, it becomes downright unbelievable. Serve it on a buffet. Or, for an elegant sit-down appetizer, slice it into individual servings and plate the slices with toast points and lemon wedges. Pictured on page 27.

Prep: 45 minutes Chill: 4$\frac{1}{2}$ hours
Makes: 16 servings

  $\frac{3}{4}$ cup water
    2 envelopes unflavored gelatin
    1 teaspoon sugar
 1$\frac{1}{4}$ cups mayonnaise or salad dressing
  $\frac{1}{4}$ cup tomato sauce
  $\frac{1}{4}$ cup lemon juice
    1 teaspoon dried dill
  $\frac{1}{4}$ teaspoon ground black pepper
    1 pound smoked salmon, flaked, with skin
       and bones removed
  $\frac{1}{2}$ cup finely chopped celery
    2 hard-cooked eggs, chopped
    2 tablespoons snipped chives
  $\frac{3}{4}$ cup whipping cream
       Thin cucumber slices (optional)
       Fresh dill (optional)
       Assorted crackers and/or
       baguette slices

1. Place water in a small saucepan. Sprinkle unflavored gelatin and sugar on the water; let stand 3 minutes to soften gelatin. Heat, stirring constantly, over medium heat until gelatin dissolves. Remove from heat.

2. In a large bowl combine mayonnaise, tomato sauce, lemon juice, dill, and pepper; stir in gelatin mixture. Chill gelatin mixture until partially set, about 30 minutes. Fold in salmon, celery, chopped hard-cooked eggs, and chives.

3. In a small bowl beat whipping cream until soft peaks form. Fold whipped cream into gelatin mixture. Pour into a 6-cup fish-shape or ring mold. Cover and chill until firm, about 4 hours.

4. To serve, unmold mousse onto tray. If desired, garnish with cucumber slices and fresh dill. Serve with assorted crackers.

Unmolding: *Set the mold in a bowl or sink filled with warm water for several seconds or until the mousse edges appear to pull away from the mold.*

Hard-Cooked Eggs: *Place eggs in a small saucepan. Add enough cold water to just cover the eggs. Bring to rapid boiling over high heat (water will have large rapidly breaking bubbles). Remove from heat, cover, and let stand for 15 minutes; drain. Run cold water over the eggs or place them in ice water until cool enough to handle; drain. To peel eggs, gently tap each egg on a countertop. Roll the egg between the palms of your hands. Peel off eggshell, starting at the large end.*

Smoked Trout Quesadillas

With cheese oozing between two warmed tortillas, quesadillas have long been an appealing snack. Here's the basic idea made elegant with goat cheese and smoked fish.

Prep: 15 minutes Cook: 3 minutes
Oven: 300°F Makes: 20 servings

   1 5.3-ounce package soft goat cheese (chèvre)
   5 8-inch flour tortillas
   8 ounces smoked trout fillets or other smoked white fish, skinned, boned, and flaked
   ¼ cup finely chopped red onion
   ¼ cup chopped roasted red sweet pepper
   ¼ teaspoon ground black pepper
      Horseradish Sauce
      Cherry tomato wedges (optional)
      Fresh cilantro (optional)

1. Spread 2 tablespoons of the goat cheese over half of each tortilla. Top with smoked fish, red onion, roasted sweet pepper, and black pepper. Fold tortillas in half, pressing gently. If desired, wrap and chill filled tortillas up to 4 hours before cooking.

2. In a 10-inch skillet cook quesadillas, 1 or 2 at a time, over medium heat for 2 to 3 minutes or until lightly browned, turning once. Remove quesadillas from skillet; place on a baking sheet. Keep warm in a 300° oven. Repeat with remaining quesadillas.

3. To serve, cut each quesadilla into 4 wedges. Top with a spoonful of Horseradish Sauce. If desired, garnish with cherry tomato wedges and cilantro.

Horseradish Sauce: *In a small bowl combine one 8-ounce carton dairy sour cream, 4 teaspoons grated fresh horseradish, 1 teaspoon finely shredded lime peel, ¼ to ½ teaspoon bottled habañero pepper sauce or other bottled hot pepper sauce, ⅛ teaspoon salt, and ⅛ teaspoon ground black pepper. Chill, covered, up to 3 days.*

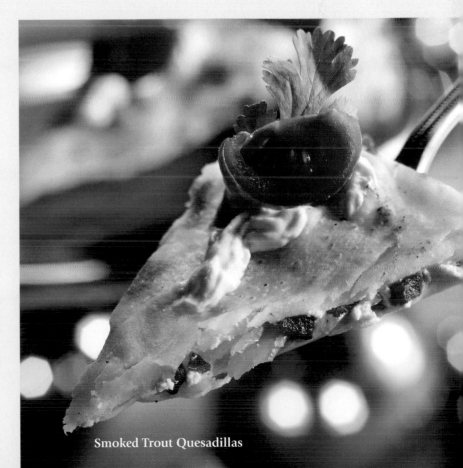

Smoked Trout Quesadillas

Crab North America has the largest variety of crabs in the world, ranging from New England's tiny rock crabs, which generally weigh less than a pound, to the giant Alaskan king crab, which can tip the scale at 20 pounds. Loved for its sweet, succulent meat, crab is second only to shrimp as America's most popular shellfish. Whole crabs are sold live, cooked, and frozen; however, in recipes such as the Divine Crab Cakes, below, cooked crabmeat is the easiest to find and use. It's available pasteurized, frozen, and canned at both well-stocked supermarkets and fish markets.

Divine Crab Cakes

This recipe hails from the low counties of North Carolina, where seafood thrives in saltwater creeks—and cooks know just what to do with it. The right blend of seasonings and a light coat of breading allow the rich, succulent flavor of crab to come through.

Prep: 15 minutes Cook: 6 minutes per batch
Makes: 8 cakes

- 2 beaten eggs
- ¾ cup soft bread crumbs
- ⅓ cup mayonnaise or salad dressing
- 1 teaspoon dry mustard
- 1 teaspoon lemon juice
- 1 teaspoon Worcestershire sauce
- ½ teaspoon salt
- ¼ teaspoon ground black pepper
- ⅛ teaspoon bottled hot pepper sauce (optional)
- 1 pound cooked crabmeat, finely flaked
- ⅓ cup fine dry bread crumbs
- 2 tablespoons cooking oil

1. In a large bowl combine the eggs, soft bread crumbs, mayonnaise, mustard, lemon juice, Worcestershire sauce, salt, black pepper, and, if desired, hot pepper sauce. Stir in crabmeat; mix well. Shape mixture into eight ½-inch patties.

2. Coat patties with the dry bread crumbs. In a large skillet heat oil over medium heat. Cook crab cakes, 4 at a time, in hot oil about 3 minutes on each side or until golden brown. Keep warm while cooking remaining crab cakes. If necessary, add additional oil to skillet.

Cajun Shrimp

A specialty of Louisiana, Cajun cooking melds French and Southern cooking styles to arrive at a lively, rustic cuisine. Although some Cajun cooking is spicy, most recipes (including this one) are more about flavor than knock-your-socks-off heat.

Prep: 25 minutes Cook: 2 minutes
Chill: 4 hours Makes: 12 servings

- ½ of a lemon
- ⅓ cup water
- 1 small onion, chopped (⅓ cup)
- 2 tablespoons lemon juice
- 1 tablespoon cooking oil
- 2 cloves garlic, minced
- 1 tablespoon Cajun seasoning
- 1½ pounds fresh or frozen peeled and deveined medium shrimp (about 2 pounds in the shell)
- ½ cup chopped green or red sweet pepper
  Lettuce leaves

1. Carefully remove peel from the lemon half, being sure not to include the bitter white pith. Cut the lemon peel into very thin strips.

2. In a large skillet combine lemon peel, water, onion, lemon juice, cooking oil, garlic, Cajun seasoning, and ¼ teaspoon *salt*. Bring to boiling. Add shrimp to skillet; stir to coat. Return to boiling, stirring frequently; reduce heat. Simmer, covered, about 2 minutes or until shrimp just turn opaque. Stir in chopped sweet pepper.

3. Transfer shrimp mixture to a glass bowl. Cover and marinate in the refrigerator for 4 hours, stirring occasionally. To serve, drain mixture well. Serve in a lettuce-lined bowl with serving picks.

Southwestern Shrimp Pâté

How do you transform a cup and a half of shrimp into a stunning appetizer for 12 guests? Serve it in this luscious pâté. Chile peppers, lemon, garlic, and cilantro make a fine backdrop for the shrimp.

Prep: 35 minutes Chill: 4 to 24 hours
Makes: 12 servings

½ cup water
1 envelope unflavored gelatin
1 8-ounce package cream cheese, softened
1 3-ounce package cream cheese, softened
½ cup dairy sour cream
⅓ cup snipped fresh cilantro
3 cloves garlic, quartered
1 small fresh red chile pepper, seeded and finely chopped (see note, page 44)
⅛ teaspoon salt
1½ cups finely chopped, cooked, peeled, and deveined shrimp (8 ounces)
2 teaspoons finely shredded lemon peel
Cooked, peeled, and deveined shrimp (optional)

Fresh cilantro sprigs (optional)
Assorted crackers

1. Line a 7×3½×3-inch loaf pan or a 3½- to 4-cup bowl or mold with plastic wrap; set aside.

2. In a small saucepan place water; sprinkle with gelatin and let stand for 5 minutes to soften gelatin. Cook and stir over low heat just until gelatin dissolves; cool slightly.

3. In a food processor bowl or blender container combine cream cheese, sour cream, the ⅓ cup cilantro, garlic, chile pepper, and salt. Cover and process or blend to combine. With processor or blender running, gradually add dissolved gelatin. Cover and process or blend until combined. Transfer cream cheese mixture to a medium bowl; stir in the 1½ cups shrimp and the lemon peel.

4. Spread shrimp mixture evenly in prepared pan. Cover and chill for 4 to 24 hours. Unmold onto a serving platter; remove plastic wrap. If desired, garnish with additional cooked shrimp and fresh cilantro sprigs. Serve with assorted crackers.

Southwestern Shrimp Pâté

Pecans The star ingredient in Pecan-Crusted Artichoke Dip, pecans are popular in Southern cooking, and there's a reason for that—they flourish in states with milder climates. While Georgia leads the country in pecan production, other Southern states grow the nut, notably Texas, where it's the state tree, and Oklahoma. Take care in storing pecans. They have a high fat content (at 70 percent, it's more than any other nut!), which accounts for their rich, buttery taste and also makes them prone to rancidity. Store unopened packages of nuts in a cool, dry place; after opening refrigerate or freeze in a tightly covered container.

Pecan-Crusted Artichoke Dip

Pecan-Crusted Artichoke Dip

Spinach-laced artichoke dips are popular everywhere; what's surprising is how easy they are to make. This one has a decidedly Southern flair with the addition of pecans.

Prep: 25 minutes Bake: 35 minutes; 6 minutes
Oven: 350°F Makes: 4 cups dip (16 to
20 servings); 72 pita dippers

1	**tablespoon butter**
½	**cup finely chopped onion**
3	**cloves garlic, minced**
4	**cups coarsely chopped fresh spinach**
1	**14-ounce can artichoke hearts, drained and chopped**
1	**8-ounce package reduced-fat cream cheese (Neufchâtel), softened**
½	**cup mayonnaise**
2	**cups shredded cheddar cheese (8 ounces)**
½	**cup grated Parmesan cheese**
2	**dashes bottled hot pepper sauce**
¼	**cup chopped pecans**
	Toasted Pita Chips

1. In a skillet melt butter over medium-high heat. Add onion and garlic; cook for 3 minutes. Add spinach; cook 3 to 5 minutes, stirring frequently. Remove from heat. Stir in artichoke hearts, cream cheese, mayonnaise, cheddar cheese, Parmesan cheese, and hot pepper sauce.

2. Transfer to an ungreased 1½-quart casserole or 1½-quart soufflé dish. Bake in a 350° oven for 25 minutes. Sprinkle with chopped pecans; bake for 10 to 15 minutes more or until heated through and pecans are toasted. Serve warm with chips.

Toasted Pita Chips: *Split 6 pitas horizontally; cut each half into 6 wedges. Arrange in a single layer on an ungreased baking sheet. Bake in a 350° oven for 6 to 10 minutes or until golden brown, turning once.*

Georgia Gold Peanuts

Sugar and citrus sweetness make one of the South's most famous nuts complement any appetizer spread. Luster dust, sold with cake decorating supplies, adds a magical sparkle.

Start to Finish: 15 minutes Makes: about 3 cups

¾ cup sugar
3 tablespoons orange juice
1 tablespoon water
2½ cups salted peanuts
1 teaspoon grated orange peel
½ teaspoon gold luster dust (optional)

1. In a medium saucepan, combine sugar, orange juice, and water. Heat to boiling. Reduce heat to medium-low; cook for 5 to 8 minutes or until syrup reaches soft-ball stage.*

2. Remove candy from heat; stir in peanuts and orange peel, stirring to coat evenly. Turn out onto waxed paper, separating nuts with a fork. Cool completely. If desired, place in a self-sealing plastic bag; add luster dust, seal, and shake to coat. Store in a sealed jar.

*Note: *The little amount of syrup in the pan makes it difficult to accurately test for soft-ball stage with a candy thermometer. To test for soft-ball stage, spoon a few drops of hot candy mixture into a cup of very cold, not icy, water. Use your fingers to form the drops into a ball. Remove ball from water; candy should instantly flatten and run between your fingers. If it doesn't, continue cooking and retesting, using fresh water and a clean spoon each time you test.*

Whiskey Laced Party Pecans

These pecans are imbued with a double-whammy of Southern pride: whiskey and bottled hot pepper sauce.

**Prep: 10 minutes Bake: 25 minutes
Oven: 300°F Makes: 4 cups**

¼ cup butter
¼ cup whiskey
3 tablespoons sugar

1 to 2 tablespoons bottled hot pepper
 sauce, or to taste
½ teaspoon salt
½ teaspoon garlic powder
4 cups pecan halves (about 1 pound)

1. In a large saucepan combine all ingredients, except pecans. Bring to boiling over medium heat; reduce heat. Boil gently, uncovered, for 3 minutes, stirring occasionally. Remove from heat. Stir in pecans; toss well to coat. Spread nuts in a single layer in a shallow baking pan. Bake in a 300° oven for 25 to 30 minutes or until nuts are crisp, stirring occasionally. Spread on foil; cool. Store in an airtight container.

Yam and Peanut Soup

Pair two Southern favorites—yams and peanuts—for a warm first course to a ham dinner, or serve it with ham sandwiches.

**Prep: 20 minutes Cook: 30 minutes
Makes: 6 first-course or side-dish servings**

3 cups peeled, sliced yams or sweet
 potatoes (about 1 pound)
¼ cup chopped onion
¼ cup chopped celery
2 tablespoons unsalted butter
4 cups reduced-sodium chicken broth
⅓ cup creamy peanut butter
¼ teaspoon ground black pepper
 Chopped peanuts (optional)
 Snipped fresh chives (optional)

1. In a large saucepan cook yams, onion, and celery in hot butter over medium heat for 5 minutes, stirring occasionally. Add broth. Bring to boiling; reduce heat. Simmer, covered, about 30 minutes or until vegetables are tender. Remove from heat; cool slightly. Transfer half the mixture to a food processor bowl or blender container. Cover; process or blend until smooth. Repeat with remaining mixture.

2. Return yam mixture to saucepan; add peanut butter and pepper. Cook and stir over medium-low heat until combined and heated through. If desired, sprinkle servings with chopped peanuts and chives; season with additional pepper.

Country Ham Gougère

Best described as a savory cream puff, gougère (goo-ZHAIR) usually is served as a baked appetizer pastry. Here the classic gets a robust Southern spin: studded with ham, kicked up with cayenne, and fried like a Southern fritter. Pictured on page 30.

Prep: 40 minutes Cook: 12 minutes
Cool: 5 minutes Oven: 300°F Makes: about 50

- ¼ **pound Smithfield ham or other country-style ham, cut into short thin strips**
- 1 **cup water**
- ½ **cup butter**
- 1 **tablespoon sugar**
- ¼ **teaspoon cayenne pepper**
- ¾ **cup all-purpose flour**
- ¼ **cup cornmeal**
- 3 **eggs**
- 8 **ounces Mimolette or sharp cheddar cheese, finely shredded**
  Cooking oil

1. In a nonstick skillet cook ham over medium heat, stirring frequently, about 10 minutes or until crisp. Drain on paper towels. Set aside.

2. In a medium saucepan combine water, butter, sugar, and cayenne pepper. Bring to boiling. Stir in flour and cornmeal; cook over medium heat until mixture forms a ball. Remove from heat. Let cool for 5 minutes.

3. Add eggs, 1 at a time, beating well with a wooden spoon after each addition. Stir in ham and cheese.

4. Heat oil in a deep saucepan or deep-fat fryer to 365°F. Drop batter into hot oil by rounded teaspoons, 5 or 6 at a time; cook about 2 minutes or until golden brown, turning once, if necessary, to brown evenly. Drain on paper towels. Keep warm in a 300° oven up to 30 minutes while frying remaining gougère.

Make-Ahead Tip: *Prepare gougère as directed. Cool, cover, and chill up to 24 hours. Before serving, arrange on a baking sheet; bake in a 350° oven for 8 to 10 minutes or until heated through.*

Mushrooms Filled with Ham and Blue Cheese

Tasty stuffed mushrooms are an all-American tradition—and a tasty way to use leftover holiday ham.

Prep: 25 minutes Bake: 13 minutes
Oven: 425°F Makes: 24 filled mushrooms

- 24 **large fresh mushrooms (about 2 inches in diameter)**
- 1 **tablespoon olive oil**
- ½ **cup finely chopped cooked ham**
- ⅓ **cup fine dry bread crumbs**
- ¼ **cup crumbled blue cheese (1 ounce)**
- 2 **tablespoons snipped fresh parsley**
- 2 **tablespoons olive oil**
- 2 **cloves garlic, minced**
- ⅛ **teaspoon cayenne pepper**

1. Wash and drain mushrooms; pat dry. Remove stems and reserve for another use. Lightly brush rounded side of the mushroom caps with the 1 tablespoon olive oil. Place mushroom caps, cavity sides up, in a shallow baking pan; set aside.

2. Combine ham, bread crumbs, blue cheese, parsley, the 2 tablespoons olive oil, garlic, and cayenne pepper in a small bowl. Spoon ham mixture into mushroom caps. If desired, cover and chill up to 12 hours.

3. Bake, uncovered, in a 425° oven for 13 to 15 minutes or until mushrooms are tender and filling is hot.

Mushrooms Filled with Ham and Blue Cheese

Sweet-and-Sour Ham Balls

Ham Folks in the ham industry distinguish between two types of ham—city ham and country ham. What's the difference? Country hams—considered higher-quality hams—are dry-cured for days, slowly smoked, and aged for 6 to 12 months. They're produced in small batches in the farmlands of such Southern states as North and South Carolina, Kentucky, Tennessee, Virginia, and Georgia. Each producer often brings its own distinct flair to the process. Mass-produced or city hams are the kind you'll most often find in the supermarket. They're injected with salt solutions and are either smoked or injected with smoke flavor.

Sweet-and-Sour Ham Balls

You can rely on cocktail-size meatballs to disappear fast on an appetizer spread. These gems veer off the beaten path with ham, pork, graham crackers, and a ginger-spiked sweet-and-sour sauce.

Prep: 20 minutes **Bake:** 15 minutes **Oven:** 350°F
Cook: 2 hours on low; 1 hour on high
Makes: 30 meatballs

- 1   beaten egg
- ½   cup graham cracker crumbs or ¼ cup fine dry bread crumbs
- 2   tablespoons milk
- ½   pound ground fully cooked ham
- ½   pound ground pork
- 1   9- or 10-ounce bottle sweet-and-sour sauce
- ⅓   cup unsweetened pineapple juice
- ⅓   cup packed brown sugar
- ½   teaspoon ground ginger

1. For meatballs, in a large bowl combine egg, cracker crumbs, and milk. Add ground ham and pork; mix well. Shape meat mixture into 30 meatballs. Place meatballs in a 15×10×1-inch baking pan. Bake in a 350° oven for 15 to 20 minutes or until done (160°F). Drain off fat.

2. Meanwhile, in a 3½- or 4-quart slow cooker stir together sweet-and-sour sauce, pineapple juice, brown sugar, and ground ginger.

3. Add browned meatballs to slow cooker. Gently stir to coat meatballs with sauce. Cover and cook on low-heat setting for 2 to 3 hours or on high-heat setting for 1 to 1½ hours. Serve immediately or keep warm on low-heat setting up to 2 hours.

41

Chunky Guacamole

Chunky Guacamole

The world probably has as many recipes for guacamole as there are cooks in Mexico and the Southwest. This chunky version gets extra zing from lime juice, and you can tailor it to your own tastes with the suggested stir-in variations.

Prep: 20 minutes Chill: 1 hour Makes: 2 cups

- 2 medium plum tomatoes, seeded and cut up
- ¼ of a small red onion, cut up
- 1 or 2 cloves garlic, peeled and halved
- 2 tablespoons lime juice
- 1 tablespoon olive oil
- ¼ teaspoon salt
- ⅛ teaspoon ground black pepper
- 2 ripe avocados, seeded, peeled, and cut up
    Tortilla chips

1. In a food processor bowl combine tomatoes, onion, garlic, lime juice, oil, salt, and pepper. Cover; process with several on/off turns until coarsely chopped.

2. Add avocados; cover and process with on/off turns just until mixture is chopped. Spoon into serving bowl; cover with plastic wrap. Chill in refrigerator up to 1 hour. Serve with tortilla chips.

Variations: *Stir in additional ingredients before chilling. Choose 1 or more of the following: 1 fresh green chile pepper or jalapeño pepper (see note, page 44), seeded and chopped; ¼ cup dairy sour cream; ¼ cup snipped fresh cilantro; ¼ to ½ teaspoon ground cumin; or ⅛ to ¼ teaspoon cayenne pepper.*

Mexicitos

These meat-filled turnovers, known in Mexico as empanaditas, brim with Southwestern flavors. Refrigerated biscuits simplify the prep.

Prep: 50 minutes Oven: 350°F
Bake: 10 minutes Makes: 40 appetizers

- 1¼ pounds lean ground beef
- 1 8-ounce can tomato sauce
- 2 teaspoons chili powder
- 2 teaspoons dried oregano, crushed

1 teaspoon garlic powder
1 tablespoon snipped fresh cilantro
2 10- to 12-ounce packages refrigerated
buttermilk biscuits (20 total)
Milk
Salsa (optional)

1. For filling, in a large skillet cook ground beef; drain off fat. Stir in tomato sauce, chili powder, oregano, and garlic powder. Bring to boiling; reduce heat. Simmer, uncovered, for 5 minutes. Remove from heat. Stir in cilantro.

2. Cut each biscuit in half horizontally. Shape each portion into a ball. On a lightly floured surface, roll each ball into a 4-inch circle. Place about 1 tablespoon of filling onto half of each circle. Fold opposite half over filling. Brush edges with some milk; seal edges with tines of a fork.

3. Place filled biscuits 1 inch apart on a large greased baking sheet. Brush tops with milk. Bake in a 350° oven for 10 to 12 minutes or until golden brown. Remove from baking sheet immediately. Cool slightly on wire rack. Serve warm. If desired, serve with salsa for dipping.

Make-Ahead Tip: *Cool completely on wire racks. Place in airtight freezer container; freeze up to 3 months. To reheat, transfer frozen Mexicitos to an ungreased baking sheet. Bake, uncovered, in a 350°F oven for 10 to 12 minutes or until heated through.*

Toasted Parmesan Squares

Chili powder or chile peppers update these classic appetizers with a Southwestern twist. Hint: Serve them hot on a pretty tray as you mingle with your guests.

Prep: 20 minutes Broil: 2 minutes
Makes: about 20 squares

¾ cup mayonnaise or salad dressing
1 medium onion, chopped (½ cup)
⅓ cup grated Parmesan cheese
¼ teaspoon salt
¼ teaspoon ground black pepper
¼ teaspoon Worcestershire sauce

⅛ teaspoon chili powder or 1 tablespoon
canned diced green chile peppers,*
drained (optional)
20 slices party rye or pumpernickel bread

1. In a bowl stir together mayonnaise, onion, cheese, salt, black pepper, Worcestershire sauce, and, if desired, chili powder or chile peppers.**

2. Place bread slices on a baking sheet; broil slices 4 inches from the heat for 1 to 2 minutes or until lightly toasted. Remove from heat; spread 1 tablespoon cheese mixture on each slice. Broil slices 1 to 2 minutes more or until topping is golden brown. Serve immediately.

*Note: *See page 44 for handling chile peppers.*

**Note: *Recipe can be prepared to this step and chilled in the refrigerator until ready to use.*

Pimiento Spread

This Southern classic is spread on crackers and tea sandwiches throughout the South. Jalapeños and pickle relish add a new kick.

Prep: 10 minutes Stand: 1 hour
Chill: 4 hours Makes: about 1¾ cups

3 cups finely shredded sharp and/or
extra-sharp cheddar cheese (12 ounces)
¼ cup mayonnaise or salad dressing
1 2-ounce jar diced pimientos, drained
1 to 2 tablespoons bottled chopped
jalapeño peppers, drained
1 tablespoon sweet pickle relish
1 teaspoon sugar (optional)
Assorted crackers

1. Allow cheese to stand, covered, at room temperature for 30 minutes; place in food processor bowl. Add mayonnaise, pimiento, jalapeño peppers, relish, and, if desired, sugar. Cover and process until smooth. Transfer to a serving bowl. Cover; chill in refrigerator at least 4 hours or up to 24 hours. Let spread stand at room temperature, covered, for 30 minutes before serving. Serve with assorted crackers.

Queso Fundido with
Corn Bread Dippers

Queso Fundido with
Corn Bread Dippers

Gathering over a flaming pot of food ensures a good time: That's the appeal of fondue. With lively chile pepper bite and crisp jicama crunch, this recipe is a Southwestern take on the popular party dish.

Prep: 1¼ hours Stand: 15 minutes
Bake: 20 minutes Oven: 425°F
Makes: 24 servings

    2 fresh poblano peppers*
    1 small red sweet pepper
    3 cups shredded Monterey Jack cheese
       (12 ounces)
    2 tablespoons all-purpose flour
    ⅓ cup finely chopped onion
    1 tablespoon butter or margarine
    ¾ cup half-and-half or light cream
    ⅓ cup finely chopped, peeled jicama
       Corn Bread Dippers

1. Quarter peppers; remove stems, seeds, and membranes.* Place pieces skin side up on foil-lined baking sheet. Bake in a 425° oven for 20 to 25 minutes or until skins are blistered and dark. Wrap peppers in foil; let stand 15 minutes. Peel skin from peppers; discard. Finely chop peppers.

2. Meanwhile, in a bowl toss together cheese and flour; set aside. In a medium saucepan cook onion in hot butter until onion is tender. Stir in half-and-half. Gradually add small amounts of the cheese mixture, stirring constantly over low heat until cheese is melted. Stir in roasted peppers and jicama; heat through.

3. Transfer cheese mixture to fondue pot or 1-quart slow cooker. Place fondue pot on burner or turn cooker to low-heat setting. Keep dip warm up to 2 hours. Serve with Corn Bread Dippers.

Corn Bread Dippers: *Prepare one 8½-ounce package corn muffin mix. Spread batter in greased 9×9×2-inch baking pan. Bake in 400° oven about 15 minutes or until golden. Cool in pan on wire rack for 10 minutes. Remove bread from pan; cool completely on rack. Cut into ½-inch slices; cut each slice in thirds. Place in a single layer on ungreased baking sheet. Bake in a 400° oven for 8 to 10 minutes or until crisp and golden, turning after 5 minutes. Cool on a wire rack. Store in airtight container up to 2 days. Makes 48 dippers.*

***Note:** Hot chile peppers, such as jalapeños and poblanos, contain volatile oils that can burn skin and eyes. Avoid direct contact with chiles as much as possible, wearing plastic gloves when you work with them. If your bare hands touch peppers, wash well with soap and water.*

Date-Sausage Bites

Dates grow abundantly in California, where cooks have come up with great ways to use them in everything from appetizers to desserts. These irresistible appetizers combine the sweet fruit with savory sausage and a dash of spice. Purchased puff pastry makes them elegant and easy.

Prep: 20 minutes Stand: 20 minutes
Bake: 20 minutes Oven: 400°F
Makes: about 27

- ½ of a 17.3-ounce package frozen puff pastry (1 sheet)
- 6 ounces uncooked maple-flavored pork sausage
- ½ cup pitted chopped dates
- ½ teaspoon garlic powder
- ¼ teaspoon dried rubbed sage or oregano, crushed
- ⅛ teaspoon crushed red pepper
- ⅛ teaspoon ground black pepper

1. Let puff pastry stand at room temperature for 20 to 30 minutes or just until thawed. Carefully unfold pastry. Cut along folds, making 3 rectangles; set aside.

2. For filling, in a small bowl combine sausage, dates, garlic powder, sage, red pepper, and black pepper. Spread about ¼ cup filling lengthwise along half of each pastry rectangle to within ½ inch of a long edge. Fold the other long side of pastry over filling; pinch edges to seal. Cut filled pastries into 1-inch pieces. Place the pieces, pastry side down, on an ungreased 15×10×1-inch baking pan. Bake in a 400° oven for 20 minutes or until golden brown. Serve warm.

Make-Ahead Tip: *To get a head start on these appetizers, fill the pastry as directed, except do not cut into pieces. Cover; chill up to 2 hours. Slice and bake as directed.*

Date-Sausage Bites

Dates While dates are native to the Middle East, the United States produces its share of the sweet, rich, sugary fruit—35 million pounds, in fact. Most American dates are grown in California; California's Coachella Valley is hailed as the Date Capital of the World. Five main varieties of California dates are available, the most popular being the sweet, delicately flavored semisoft Deglet Noor, which represents 90 percent of the state's crop. Less common, but prized by date lovers, is the large premium Medjool date, a gourmet variety that's worth seeking out when the date will be stuffed or otherwise shown off in its full, plump glory. Any variety will do for the lovely Date-Sausage Puffs. Store dried dates in a tightly closed container in the refrigerator for several months or for up to a year in the freezer.

Regional Takes on Breakfast and Brunch

WHETHER YOU'RE HOSTING A HOUSE filled with overnight guests or opening your doors to friends and neighbors, one of the merriest (and easiest!) ways to gather people around the table is over a breakfast, brunch, or luncheon. This year, strike out of the ordinary! Call on luscious smoked salmon to put a Northwest spin on eggs Benedict, rich crab from the East to make the quiche extra luscious, and spicy chorizo from the Southwest to vitalize an egg casserole. You'll find these and other ways to brighten the occasion with fascinating foods from across the country.

Salmon and Eggs Benedict
(recipe, page 57)

Cranberry Strata

Cranberries Grown in freshwater bogs throughout the northern U.S., cranberries are credited with myriad health benefits—from improving mood to reversing memory loss. We can't vouch for all their alleged benefits, but we agree the bright, festive fruit brings a merry sweet-tart zing to such recipes as Cranberry Strata. When selecting fresh berries, choose those that are shiny, plump, and bright red. Refrigerate, tightly wrapped, up to 2 months.

Cranberry Strata

Strata is Italian for "layers." To American cooks, strata roughly translates to "a terrific and terrifically easy crowd-pleasing brunch dish made the night before." Many varieties of this ever-popular dish exist. Here cranberries and maple syrup add irresistible sweet-tart layers.

Prep: 25 minutes Bake: 65 minutes
Stand: 10 minutes Chill: 8 hours
Oven: 350°F Makes: 9 to 12 servings

  12 ounces crusty French bread or
      sourdough bread, torn into 1-inch
      pieces (8 cups)
   1 8-ounce package cream cheese
  ½ cup dried cranberries
   6 eggs
  2¼ cups milk
  ⅓ cup pure maple syrup or
      maple-flavored syrup
  ½ teaspoon ground cinnamon or
      ground nutmeg
      Orange Sauce

1. In a greased 2-quart rectangular baking dish arrange half the bread pieces.

2. Cut cream cheese into ½-inch slices. Arrange on bread in baking dish. Sprinkle cranberries on bread; top with remaining bread pieces.

3. In a medium bowl beat together eggs, milk, and maple syrup. Pour over bread and cranberries in baking dish. Sprinkle with cinnamon. Lightly press down with back of spoon to saturate bread with egg mixture. Cover and chill in refrigerator at least 8 hours or up to 24 hours.

4. Bake strata, covered, in a 350° oven for 45 minutes. Uncover; bake for 20 minutes more.

Let stand for 10 minutes before serving. Serve warm with Orange Sauce.

Orange Sauce: *In a small saucepan combine 4 teaspoons cornstarch and 1 tablespoon sugar. Stir in 1¼ cups orange juice. Cook and stir over medium heat until thickened and bubbly. Add ½ cup snipped dried cranberries and 1 tablespoon butter or margarine; cook and stir for 2 minutes more. Serve warm.*

Blueberry-Cornmeal Pancakes

Blueberries thrive in the northern United States and are in season from May to early October. Fortunately, frozen blueberries work well in this recipe, so you can serve this dish as a leisurely breakfast during the holidays.

Prep: 10 minutes Cook: 4 minutes per pancake
Makes: 8 to 10 pancakes

- 1 cup all-purpose flour
- 2 tablespoons cornmeal
- 1 tablespoon sugar
- 1 teaspoon baking powder
- ½ teaspoon baking soda
- ¼ teaspoon salt
- ¼ teaspoon ground cinnamon
- 1 beaten egg
- 1 cup buttermilk or sour milk*
- 2 tablespoons cooking oil
- 1 cup fresh or frozen blueberries
     Butter and/or maple or blueberry-flavored syrup (optional)

1. In a medium bowl combine flour, cornmeal, sugar, baking powder, baking soda, salt, and cinnamon. Make a well in the center; set aside.

2. In another medium bowl stir together the egg, buttermilk, and oil. Add egg mixture all at once to flour mixture. Stir just until moistened (batter should be lumpy). Gently fold in blueberries.

3. For each pancake, pour or spread about ¼ cup of the batter into a 4-inch circle onto a hot, lightly greased griddle or heavy skillet. Cook over medium heat about 2 minutes on each side or until pancakes are golden brown, turning to second sides when pancakes have bubbly surfaces and edges are slightly dry. Serve warm. If desired, pass butter and/or syrup.

*Note: *To make 1 cup sour milk, place 1 tablespoon lemon juice or vinegar in a glass measuring cup. Add enough milk to make 1 cup total; stir. Let mixture stand for 5 minutes before using.*

Blueberry-Cornmeal Pancakes

Gingerbread Waffles

butter. Remove from heat. Stir in baking soda. Add molasses mixture to flour mixture along with sour milk and beaten eggs. Stir just until moistened (batter will be lumpy).

2. Spread about 1 cup batter onto preheated, lightly greased waffle baker. Close lid quickly; do not open until done. Bake according to manufacturer's directions, using the light setting, if available. When done, use a fork to carefully lift waffle off grid. Repeat with remaining batter. Serve warm. If desired, sprinkle with powdered sugar and serve with maple syrup and/or fruit.

*Note: *To make sour milk, place 2 teaspoons lemon juice or vinegar in glass measuring cup. Add enough milk to make ⅔ cup total liquid; stir. Let stand for 5 minutes before using.*

Crab Chantilly

Crab is harvested along the Eastern Seaboard, and this elegant lunch entrée is reminiscent of something you'd enjoy in a gracious dining room in the Carolinas. It's a saucy dish, so serve it with plenty of crusty Italian or French bread. A crisp green salad makes a nice complement.

Prep: 15 minutes Broil: 2 minutes
Makes: 4 to 6 main-dish servings

  1 **pound fresh asparagus spears or one 10-ounce package frozen asparagus spears**
  2 **tablespoons chopped green onion (1)**
  2 **tablespoons butter or margarine**
  1 **tablespoon all-purpose flour**
  ¼ **teaspoon salt**
      Dash cayenne pepper
  1 **cup half-and-half or light cream**
  ¼ **cup mayonnaise or salad dressing (optional)**
  1 **pound cooked crabmeat or two 8-ounce packages flake-style imitation crabmeat***
  1 **tablespoon dry sherry or dry vermouth**
  ¼ **cup grated Parmesan cheese (1 ounce)**

1. Trim fresh asparagus. In a covered medium saucepan cook fresh asparagus in a small amount

Gingerbread Waffles

Made from sugarcane and sugar beets, molasses has been a staple of New England cookery since Colonial times and has made its way into many of the region's most famous specialties. Its sweetness is a welcome addition to waffles, a beloved morning treat.

Prep: 10 minutes Cook: Per waffle baker instructions Makes: 12 (4-inch) waffles

  2 **cups all-purpose flour**
  1 **teaspoon ground ginger**
  ½ **teaspoon ground cinnamon**
  1 **cup molasses**
  ½ **cup butter or margarine**
  1 **teaspoon baking soda**
  ⅔ **cup sour milk***
  2 **beaten eggs**
      Sifted powdered sugar, maple syrup, and fruit, such as strawberries and/or orange segments (optional)

1. In a bowl combine flour, ginger, ½ teaspoon *salt*, and cinnamon; make a well in the center; set aside. In a medium saucepan combine molasses and butter. Bring to boiling, stirring to melt

of boiling salted water for 4 to 6 minutes or until crisp-tender. Drain. (For frozen asparagus, cook according to package directions.)

2. In a medium saucepan, cook green onion in hot butter until tender. Stir in flour, salt, and cayenne pepper. Add half-and-half. Cook and stir over medium heat until thickened and bubbly. Remove from heat. If desired, stir in mayonnaise. Stir in crabmeat and sherry. Arrange asparagus spears in a 2-quart square baking dish. Spoon crab mixture over asparagus. Sprinkle Parmesan cheese over all.

3. Broil 4 inches from heat for 2 to 3 minutes or until lightly browned and heated through. Serve immediately.

*Note: *Cooked crabmeat is available frozen, canned, or refrigerated (as a pasteurized product); you can use any of these products. One pound cooked crabmeat is about 4 cups. Canned crabmeat usually is available in 6-ounce cans (4¼ ounces drained).*

Crab Quiche

Here's another crab-studded specialty culled from the Eastern Seaboard. While quiche is sometimes thought of as a ladies' luncheon specialty, this one—with its creamy filling and dash of vermouth—pleases all appetites. Serve with a green salad topped with sparkling citrus fruit.

Prep: 10 minutes Oven: 375°F
Bake: 30 minutes Stand: 10 minutes
Makes: 8 main-dish servings

    Baked Pastry Shell
  3 tablespoons finely chopped green onions
  1 tablespoon butter or margarine
  3 eggs
  ½ pound cooked crabmeat (2 cups) or one 6- to 8-ounce package flake-style imitation crabmeat
  1 cup half-and-half, light cream, or milk
  3 tablespoons dry vermouth (optional)
  1 tablespoon tomato paste
  1 teaspoon salt*

  ¼ teaspoon ground black pepper
  ½ cup shredded Swiss cheese (2 ounces)

1. Prepare Baked Pastry Shell; set aside. In a small skillet, cook onion in hot butter until tender. Remove from heat.

2. In a medium bowl beat eggs slightly with a fork. Stir in crabmeat, half-and-half, vermouth (if desired), tomato paste, salt, and pepper. Stir in onion mixture. Pour egg and onion mixture into pastry shell. Sprinkle with cheese.

3. Bake quiche in a 375° oven about 30 minutes or until a knife inserted near center comes out clean. Let stand for 10 minutes before serving. Cut into wedges to serve.

Baked Pastry Shell: *In a large bowl stir together 1¼ cups all-purpose flour and ¼ teaspoon salt. Cut in ⅓ cup shortening. Moisten dough with 4 to 5 tablespoons cold water total, adding 1 tablespoon water at a time and tossing with a fork. On a lightly floured surface, roll dough into a 12-inch circle. Ease pastry into a 9-inch pie plate. Trim pastry to ½ inch beyond edge of pie plate. Fold under extra pastry; crimp edge. Prick bottom and side of pastry. Line pastry with a double thickness of foil. Bake in a 450° oven for 8 minutes. Remove foil. Bake for 5 to 6 minutes more or until golden brown. Cool on a wire rack.*

*Note: *If using imitation crabmeat, which is high in sodium, you may cut the salt in the quiche filling to ½ teaspoon.*

Crab Quiche

Creamy Ham and Egg Bake

Wisconsin is often called "the dairy state," and this creamy, cheesy dish is right at home on tables there. It's a great recipe to make for a holiday breakfast buffet: It serves 12, and you can assemble it the night before.

Prep: 30 minutes Chill: 2 hours
Bake: 50 minutes Oven: 350°F
Makes: 12 servings

- 10 eggs
- ¼ teaspoon salt
- 2 tablespoons butter or margarine
- 3 tablespoons butter or margarine
- 3 tablespoons all-purpose flour
- ¼ teaspoon ground black pepper
- 1¾ cups milk
- 1½ cups process Gruyère or Swiss cheese, cut up (6 ounces)
- 2 teaspoons prepared mustard
- 2 16-ounce packages frozen loose-pack broccoli, corn, and red peppers, thawed and well drained
- 6 ounces fully cooked ham, cut into bite-size strips (about 1 cup)
- 2 ounces process Gruyère or Swiss cheese, shredded (½ cup)

1. In a medium mixing bowl beat together eggs and salt with a rotary beater. In a 10-inch skillet melt the 2 tablespoons butter over medium heat. Pour in egg mixture. Cook without stirring until mixture begins to set on the bottom and around the edges. Using a large spoon or spatula, lift and fold partially cooked eggs so uncooked portion flows underneath. Continue cooking over medium heat about 4 minutes total or until eggs are cooked through and still glossy and moist. Immediately remove eggs from heat; set aside.

2. For sauce, in a 4-quart Dutch oven melt the 3 tablespoons butter. Stir in flour and pepper. Add milk all at once. Cook and stir until thickened and bubbly. Add the 1½ cups cheese and the mustard, stirring until cheese is melted.

3. Stir vegetables and ham into the cheese mixture, then gently fold in eggs. Turn mixture into a 2-quart rectangular baking dish. Cover and chill for 2 to 24 hours.

4. Bake, covered, in a 350° oven for 45 minutes or until heated through, gently stirring after 15 minutes. Remove from oven and stir gently. Sprinkle with the ½ cup cheese. Bake about 5 minutes more or until cheese is melted.

Pork-Spinach Pie

With a super-robust filling of pork and stuffing, this Midwestern-style bake is more like a casserole than a dainty quiche—it's a deliciously hearty brunch dish. Cut into thin wedges, it makes a nice potluck dish as well.

Prep: 40 minutes Bake: 50 minutes
Oven: 450°F/325°F Stand: 10 minutes
Makes: 6 servings

- ½ of a 10-ounce package frozen chopped spinach, thawed
  Pastry for Single-Crust Pie (see page 78)
- 1 cup shredded Monterey Jack cheese or cheddar cheese (4 ounces)
- 8 ounces bulk pork sausage
- ½ cup herb-seasoned stuffing mix
- 3 beaten eggs
- 1¼ cups milk

1. Drain spinach well, pressing out excess liquid; set aside. Prepare pastry. On a lightly floured surface, use your hands to slightly flatten dough. Roll dough from center to edges into a circle about 13 inches in diameter. To transfer pastry, wrap it around the rolling pin. Unroll pastry into a 9-inch pie plate. Ease pastry into pie plate without stretching it. Trim pastry to ½-inch beyond edge of pie plate. Fold under extra pastry. Crimp edge as desired. Do not prick pastry. Line unpricked pastry shell with a double thickness of foil. Bake in a 450° oven for 8 minutes; remove foil. Bake for 4 to 5 minutes more or until pastry is set and dry. Remove from oven. Sprinkle cheese in bottom of partially baked pie shell; set aside. Reduce oven temperature to 325°.

2. Meanwhile, in a large skillet cook sausage until brown. Drain off fat. Stir stuffing mix and spinach into sausage in skillet. Spoon sausage mixture over cheese in pie shell. In a medium bowl stir

Winter Fruit Cup

together eggs and milk. Pour egg mixture over sausage mixture.

3. Bake pie, uncovered, in a 325° oven for 50 to 55 minutes or until a knife inserted near center comes out clean. Let stand for 10 minutes before serving. Cut into wedges to serve.

Winter Fruit Cup

The creamy brown sugar and sour cream topping ushers winter fruit into the realm of lusciousness.

Prep: 30 minutes Chill: 2 hours
Makes: 6 servings

- 4 **medium oranges, peeled and sectioned**
- 3 **medium apples, cored and chopped (remove peel, if desired)**
- 2 **large grapefruit, peeled and sectioned**
- ¼ **cup granulated sugar**
- ¼ **cup butter or margarine**
- ½ **cup packed brown sugar**
- 1 **8-ounce carton dairy sour cream**
- 1 **teaspoon vanilla**
  Brown sugar (optional)

1. In a large bowl combine oranges, apples, grapefruit, and granulated sugar; toss to mix. Cover and refrigerate fruit mixture for 2 to 4 hours, stirring occasionally.

2. For sauce, in a small saucepan melt butter over medium-low heat. Stir in the ½ cup brown sugar. Cook and stir until sugar dissolves and mixture bubbles. Remove from heat. Gradually stir in sour cream and vanilla. Serve warm sauce over chilled fruit. Sprinkle each serving with additional brown sugar, if desired.

Skillet Migas

Chorizo A boldly seasoned pork sausage, chorizo stars in Skillet Migas. Mexican chorizo, which is popular in Tex-Mex and Southwestern cooking, is made with fresh pork, while Spanish chorizo is made with smoked pork. Find chorizo at Hispanic markets and well-stocked supermarkets. Or make some yourself—it requires only fresh pork and a few seasonings. See the recipe, opposite.

Skillet Migas

Migas is Spanish for "crumbs." This skillet egg casserole, with crumbled tortilla chips scattered throughout, is popular in Texas.

Prep: 30 minutes Bake: 30 minutes
Oven: 350°F Makes: 8 to 10 servings

- 8 ounces Homemade Chorizo (recipe, opposite), other spicy fresh sausage, or purchased chorizo
- ½ cup chopped green sweet pepper
- ¼ cup chopped red onion
- 2 cloves garlic, minced
- 5 large, slightly beaten eggs
- 1½ cups lightly crushed corn tortilla chips
- ½ cup bottled salsa
- 1 small tomato, seeded and chopped (⅓ cup) (optional)
- 1 4½-ounce can diced green chile peppers, drained (optional)
- 3 tablespoons snipped fresh cilantro
- 1½ cups shredded cheddar cheese (6 ounces)
  Dairy sour cream
  Lime wedges

1. In 12-inch ovenproof skillet combine sausage, sweet pepper, onion, and garlic. Cook over medium heat until sausage is brown and vegetables are tender. Drain off fat.

2. In a large bowl stir together eggs, crushed chips, salsa, tomato (if desired), green chiles (if desired), cilantro, and 1 cup of the cheese. Stir in drained sausage mixture. Pour into skillet. Bake in a 350° oven for 20 minutes or until egg mixture is almost set. Sprinkle with remaining cheese; bake for 10 minutes more or until cheese is lightly golden and egg mixture is set and shiny. Cut into wedges; top with a spoonful of sour cream. Serve with lime wedges.

Southwestern Quiche

Prep: 30 minutes Bake: 40 minutes
Stand: 15 minutes Oven: 350°F
Makes: 6 servings

- ½ of an 11-ounce package piecrust mix (1 cup)
- 1 teaspoon chili powder
- 2 tablespoons cold water
- ¾ cup shredded cheddar cheese
- ½ cup shredded Monterey Jack cheese
- 3 beaten eggs
- 1½ cups half-and-half or light cream
- 1 4½-ounce can diced green chile peppers, drained
- 1 2¼-ounce can sliced ripe olives, drained
- 2 tablespoons chopped green onion (1)
- ¼ teaspoon salt
- ¼ teaspoon ground white pepper
  Dairy sour cream (optional)
  Bottled salsa (optional)
  Sliced green onions (optional)

1. In a medium bowl stir together piecrust mix and chili powder; stir in cold water. Shape into a ball. On a lightly floured surface, slightly flatten dough. Roll from center to 12-inch-diameter circle. Wrap pastry around rolling pin; unroll into 9-inch pie plate without stretching. Trim pastry ½ inch beyond edge of pie plate; fold under extra pastry; crimp as desired. Combine cheeses; sprinkle evenly into the pastry-lined pie plate.

2. In a medium bowl combine beaten eggs, half-and-half, chile peppers, olives, 2 tablespoons green onion, salt, and white pepper; pour over cheese. Bake in a 350° oven for 40 to 45 minutes or until a knife inserted off-center comes out clean. Let stand for 15 minutes. If desired, serve with sour cream, salsa, and sliced green onions.

Homemade Chorizo

Use this Mexican-style chorizo in Skillet Migas, opposite, and in enchiladas or tacos.

Prep: 15 minutes Makes: 1 pound

- 4 dried ancho or New Mexico red chile peppers, washed and patted dry (see note, page 44)* or 2 tablespoons red chili powder
- 1 pound ground pork
- ¼ cup finely chopped onion
- 3 cloves garlic, minced
- 1 teaspoon cumin seeds, crushed
- 1 teaspoon dried oregano, crushed
- ½ teaspoon salt
- ½ teaspoon ground black pepper
- 1 tablespoon apple cider vinegar or lime juice

1. If using dried chile peppers, remove stems and seeds. Place peppers in a blender container or food processor bowl. Cover and blend or process until very finely chopped.

2. For chorizo, in a large bowl combine chopped dried chile peppers, ground pork, onion, garlic, cumin, oregano, salt, pepper, and vinegar. Crumble chorizo into a large skillet; cook and stir over medium heat until browned.

*Note: *To make dried red chile peppers easy to grind and to bring out flavor, place on a baking sheet; bake in a 350° oven for 1 to 2 minutes until pliable and fragrant. Do not deeply inhale chile pepper fumes.*

Make-Ahead Tip: *Wrap chorizo in plastic freezer wrap and foil. Freeze up to 3 months.*

Southwestern Quiche

King Ranch Casserole

King Ranch Casserole

The brunch casserole is a well-known specialty in the Lone Star State and a hearty dish to serve cowboys with big appetites.

Prep: 50 minutes Bake: 35 minutes
Stand: 10 minutes Oven: 350°F
Makes: 12 servings

 2 tomatillos, husks removed, rinsed, and finely chopped (about ½ cup)
 1 large onion, chopped (1 cup)
 1 clove garlic, minced
 2 tablespoons cooking oil
 2 4-ounce jars diced pimiento, drained
 2 4-ounce cans diced green chile peppers
 2 tablespoons finely chopped, seeded jalapeño peppers (about 2 peppers) (see note, page 44)

 12 6-inch corn tortillas
     Cooking oil
 ¼ cup butter or margarine
 ¼ cup all-purpose flour
 4 teaspoons chili powder
 1 teaspoon dried oregano, crushed
 ¼ teaspoon salt
    Dash ground black pepper
 2 cups chicken broth or one 14-ounce can chicken broth
 1 8-ounce carton dairy sour cream or fat-free dairy sour cream
 3 cups shredded cooked chicken or turkey (1 pound)
 2 cups shredded mozzarella cheese or Monterey Jack cheese (8 ounces)
    Chopped fresh tomato or tomato wedges (optional)
    Fresh cilantro or parsley (optional)

1. In a medium saucepan cook tomatillos, onion, and garlic in the 2 tablespoons cooking oil until vegetables are tender. Remove from heat; stir in drained pimiento, chile peppers, and jalapeño peppers. Set aside.

2. In a medium skillet cook tortillas, 1 at a time, in about ¼ inch cooking oil over medium-high heat until tortillas are crisp, turning once (20 to 30 seconds per side). Drain on paper towels; set aside.

3. For sauce, in another saucepan melt the butter; stir in flour, chili powder, oregano, salt, and black pepper. Add chicken broth. Cook and stir until thickened and bubbly. Cook and stir for 1 minute more; remove from heat. Stir in sour cream.

4. Arrange 6 of the tortillas, overlapping slightly, in an ungreased 3-quart rectangular baking dish. Top with half the chicken, half the vegetables, half the sauce, and half the cheese. Repeat layers.

5. Cover loosely with foil. Bake in a 350° oven for 35 to 40 minutes or until heated through. Let stand for 10 minutes; cut into squares to serve. If desired, garnish with fresh tomato and cilantro.

Make-Ahead Tip: *Refrigerate tomato mixture, tightly covered, up to 1 day. Store toasted tortillas in airtight container at room temperature up to 1 day.*

Salmon and Eggs Benedict

Eggs Benedict is a lavish brunch dish—and variations of it seem endless. In this recipe, smoked salmon, a popular ingredient in the Pacific Northwest, stands in for Canadian bacon, and the eggs are scrambled rather than poached. Pictured on page 47.

Prep: 30 minutes Bake: 25 minutes Oven: 350°F
Makes: 6 servings

- 1 1⅛-ounce or .9-ounce envelope hollandaise sauce mix (to make about 1¼ cups sauce)
- 2 tablespoons capers, drained
- ½ teaspoon finely shredded lemon peel
- 3 **English muffins, split and toasted**
- 6 **ounces thinly sliced, smoked salmon (lox-style)**
- 6 **eggs**
- ¼ **cup milk**
- ⅛ **teaspoon ground black pepper**
- 2 **tablespoons butter or margarine**
- ¾ **cup soft bread crumbs (1 slice)**
     Snipped fresh chives (optional)

1. Prepare sauce mix according to package directions. Stir in capers and lemon peel. Spread about ½ cup of the sauce on the bottom of a 2-quart rectangular baking dish. Cover remaining sauce and set aside. Arrange muffins, cut sides up, on sauce in baking dish. Divide salmon in 6 equal portions. Place salmon, folding as necessary, on each muffin half.

2. In a bowl beat together eggs, milk, and pepper. In a large skillet melt 1 tablespoon of the butter over medium heat. Pour egg mixture into skillet. Cook, without stirring, until mixture begins to set on top and around edges. Using a spatula, lift and fold partially cooked eggs so uncooked portion flows underneath. Continue cooking for 3 to 4 minutes or until eggs are cooked but still moist.

3. Spoon eggs on muffins with salmon, dividing evenly. Spoon remaining sauce on eggs.

4. For crumb topping, in a skillet melt the remaining butter. Add bread crumbs, tossing lightly to coat. Sprinkle crumb topping over sauce on muffins.

5. Bake, uncovered, in a 350° oven 25 minutes or until heated through. If desired, sprinkle with snipped chives.

Make-Ahead Tip: *Prepare sauce and egg mixture for Salmon and Eggs Benedict as directed. Cover and chill the sauce and egg mixture separately in the refrigerator overnight. Prepare crumb topping. Cover and chill in the refrigerator overnight. To serve, assemble egg stacks as directed. Sprinkle eggs with crumb topping. Bake and serve as directed.*

Easy Eggs Benedict with Canadian Bacon: *Prepare as directed, except substitute 6 ounces Canadian-style bacon for the smoked salmon.*

The Coast-to-Coast Breadbasket

WHY SERVE THE USUAL DINNER rolls when you can make them distinctively Southwestern with cornmeal and cheese? Imagine how good sticky rolls taste with Southern pecans and coconut in the mix. If you think that's really something, you'll be amazed what happens when you infuse Danish pastries with irresistibly tart and tingly Key lime flavors! Tweak traditional biscuit, roll, and quick-bread recipes by adding a range of American ingredients. You and your guests will see just how fascinating holiday breadbaskets can be.

Fruit-and-Nut Ring (recipe, page 66)

pieces are the size of small peas. Make a well in the center; add yeast mixture along with the beaten eggs. Stir until all the dough is moistened. Transfer dough to a lightly greased bowl. Cover and let rise in a warm place until double (1 to 1¼ hours).

3. Lightly grease baking sheets; set aside. Turn out dough onto a well-floured surface. Knead 10 to 12 times. Roll dough to ¼-inch thickness. Use floured round cutters to cut twenty-four 2½-inch rounds and twenty-four 2-inch rounds. Place larger rounds on prepared baking sheets. Brush tops with melted butter. Top each round with a smaller round, stacking slightly off-center. Cover and let rise in a warm place for 30 minutes.

4. Brush the tops of biscuits with a mixture of egg yolk and the 1 teaspoon of milk. Bake in a 400° oven for 13 to 15 minutes or until tops are golden. Serve warm.

Quaker Bonnet Biscuits

If you love old-fashioned heirloom recipes, these New England biscuits will be your cup of tea. Shaped like hats worn by Quaker women in the early 1800s, these biscuits evolved from a recipe in Mary at the Farm, *a 1915 cookbook. The freshly revised technique keeps the homespun appeal intact.*

Prep: 20 minutes Bake: 1½ hours
Bake: 13 minutes Oven: 400°F Makes: 24

      1⅓ cups warm milk (105°F to 115°F)
      1   package active dry yeast
      4   cups all-purpose flour
      1   teaspoon salt
      ⅓   cup butter, shortening, or lard
      2   eggs, beaten
      1   tablespoon butter, melted
      1   egg yolk
      1   teaspoon milk

1. In a bowl combine warm milk and yeast; let stand about 5 minutes for yeast to soften.

2. In a large bowl combine flour and salt. Using a pastry blender, cut in the ⅓ cup butter until

Blueberry-Corn Bread Mini Loaves

Thanks to deep blue berries and yellow cornmeal, these loaves have lovely flavor and color. To present the loaves as a gift, consider including a jar of Lemon Butter and advise the recipient that quick breads are tastiest the day after baking.

Prep: 20 minutes Bake: 35 minutes
Oven: 350°F Makes: 3 loaves (30 servings)

      1½ cups all-purpose flour
      1½ cups yellow cornmeal
      ¾   cup sugar
      1   tablespoon baking powder
      ½   teaspoon salt
      ½   teaspoon finely shredded lemon peel
      2   eggs
      1¼ cups milk
      ¼   cup cooking oil
      1   cup fresh or frozen blueberries
          Lemon Glaze (optional)
          Lemon Butter

1. Grease bottoms and about ½ inch up the sides of three 5¾×3×2-inch loaf pans; set aside. In a

large bowl combine the flour, cornmeal, sugar, baking powder, salt, and lemon peel. Make a well in the center of the flour mixture; set aside.

2. In a medium bowl combine the eggs, milk, and oil. Add egg mixture all at once to flour mixture. Stir just until moistened. Fold in blueberries. Spoon batter into prepared loaf pans.

3. Bake in a 350° oven for 35 to 40 minutes or until a wooden toothpick inserted near center comes out clean. Cool in pans on wire racks for 10 minutes. Remove from pans. Cool completely. Wrap and store loaves overnight. If desired, drizzle each loaf with Lemon Glaze. Serve with Lemon Butter.

Lemon Glaze: *In a small bowl stir together ¾ cup sifted powdered sugar, 2 teaspoons lemon juice, and 2 to 3 teaspoons water until of glazing consistency.*

Lemon Butter: *In a small mixing bowl beat ½ cup softened butter, 1 tablespoon sifted powdered sugar, and 1 teaspoon finely shredded lemon peel with an electric mixer until smooth. Cover and chill at least 1 hour to allow flavors to blend. Let stand at room temperature about 30 minutes before serving. Makes ½ cup.*

Lemon-Thyme Scones

Snip a little fresh thyme, grate some lemon peel, and add cream for a sprightly rich scone that veers well off the beaten path. These tender, flaky gems are best served warm, so if you give them as gifts, include directions to wrap in foil and reheat in a 350°F oven for 10 minutes.

Prep: 20 minutes **Bake:** 15 minutes
Oven: 400°F **Makes:** 10 scones

- 2 cups all-purpose flour
- 2 tablespoons granulated sugar
- 1 tablespoon baking powder
- 2 teaspoons snipped fresh thyme (optional)

- 2 teaspoons finely shredded lemon peel
- ¼ teaspoon salt
- 6 tablespoons butter
- 1 egg, slightly beaten
- ½ cup whipping cream
- 2 tablespoons whipping cream
-    Coarse sugar
-    Lemon Butter (see recipe, left)

1. In a large bowl combine flour, granulated sugar, baking powder, thyme (if desired), lemon peel, and salt. Using a pastry blender, cut in butter until the mixture resembles coarse crumbs. In a small bowl or measuring cup combine egg and the ½ cup whipping cream. Add to flour mixture. Stir just until moistened.

2. On a lightly floured surface knead dough 10 to 12 strokes. Pat into a 7-inch circle about 1 inch thick. Cut into 10 wedges. Place 1 inch apart on a greased baking sheet. Brush with the 2 tablespoons cream; sprinkle with coarse sugar. Bake in a 400° oven for 15 to 20 minutes or until golden brown. Serve warm with Lemon Butter.

Blueberry-Corn Bread Mini Loaves

Key Lime
Danish Pastries

Key Limes Smaller and more yellow than Persian limes, Key limes are grown in the Florida Keys. You might have to shop at a specialty store to find them, and because of their size you'll likely need more of them. Are they worth the time and trouble? While purists believe you can't have Key lime pie or Key lime anything without Key limes, the juice squeezed from fresh Persian limes does just fine in Key Lime Danish Pastries.

Key Lime Danish Pastries

Tart limes paired with a rich dairy filling produce a match made in heaven—as anyone who has tasted Key lime pie knows! The concept is just as sublime in a sweet roll. Hint: These also freeze well; see note, opposite.

Prep: 45 minutes Rise: 1 hour
Bake: 15 minutes Oven: 375°F
Makes: 24 pastries

6¼ to 6¾ cups all-purpose flour
1½ cups granulated sugar
2 packages active dry yeast
1½ teaspoons salt
1 cup milk
1 cup water
½ cup butter
1 egg
1 8-ounce package cream cheese, softened
½ teaspoon finely shredded lime peel
3 tablespoons lime juice
¾ cup sifted powdered sugar
1 teaspoon butter, melted

1. In a large mixing bowl combine 2 cups of the flour, ½ cup of the granulated sugar, the yeast, and salt; set aside. In a small saucepan heat and stir the milk, water, and the ½ cup butter just until warm (120°F to 130°F) and butter is almost melted. Add to flour mixture; add egg. Beat with an electric mixer on low to medium speed for 30 seconds, scraping side of bowl constantly. Beat on high speed for 3 minutes. Using a wooden spoon, stir in as much of the remaining flour as you can.

2. Turn out dough onto a lightly floured surface. Knead in enough of the remaining flour to make a moderately stiff dough that is smooth and elastic (6 to 8 minutes total). Shape into a ball. Place in a greased bowl; turn once to grease surface. Cover and let rise in a warm place until double (about 1 hour). Punch dough down. Turn out onto a floured surface. Divide in half. Cover; let rest for 10 minutes.

3. For filling, in a small bowl stir together cream cheese, lime peel, 2 tablespoons of the lime juice, and ½ cup of the granulated sugar; set aside.

4. For icing, in another small bowl stir together the powdered sugar, the remaining lime juice, and the 1 teaspoon butter; set aside. Lightly grease baking sheets; set aside.

5. On a floured surface, roll each half of dough into a 14×9-inch rectangle. Top each with ¼ cup of the granulated sugar. Starting from a long side, roll up dough; seal seams. Cut each roll into 12 slices; arrange slices 2 inches apart on prepared baking sheets. Make an indentation in each slice; fill each indentation with a scant tablespoon of the filling. Bake rolls in a 375° oven for 15 to 18 minutes or until golden brown. Remove from baking sheets; cool slightly. Drizzle warm pastries with icing. Serve warm.

Note: *If desired, freeze, covered, in layers separated by waxed paper in an airtight container. Thaw at room temperature.*

Cranberry-Sweet Potato Bread

Sweet-tart cranberries brighten the earthy flavor of sweet potatoes in this distinctive bread. Take whole loaves to share at work (it goes great with coffee!) or make smaller loaves to present as gifts.

Prep: 30 minutes Bake: 1 hour
Oven: 350°F Makes: 36 servings

   3½ cups all-purpose flour
   1⅔ cups sugar
   2 teaspoons baking soda
   1 teaspoon baking powder
   1 teaspoon pumpkin pie spice
   ¾ teaspoon salt
   2 cups mashed, cooked sweet potatoes
      (about 1½ pounds)
   1 16-ounce can whole cranberry sauce
   4 slightly beaten eggs
   ⅔ cup cooking oil
   ¾ cup chopped pecans
      Orange Glaze

1. Grease the bottom and ½ inch up the sides of two 9×5×3-inch loaf pans or four 7½×3½×2-inch loaf pans; set aside.

2. In an extra-large bowl combine flour, sugar, baking soda, baking powder, pumpkin pie spice, and salt; set aside.

3. In a large bowl combine sweet potatoes, cranberry sauce, eggs, and oil. Add egg mixture all at once to flour mixture; stir just until moistened. Fold in pecans. Spoon batter into prepared pans.

4. Bake in a 350° oven about 1 hour for the 9×5×3-inch loaf pans or 40 to 45 minutes for the 7½×3½×2-inch loaf pans or until a wooden toothpick inserted near center comes out clean. Cool in pans on wire racks for 10 minutes. Remove from pans. Cool completely on wire racks. Wrap in plastic wrap; store overnight before slicing. Just before serving, drizzle with Orange Glaze.

Orange Glaze: *In a small bowl stir together 1 cup sifted powdered sugar and ¼ cup frozen orange juice concentrate, thawed.*

Cranberry-Sweet
Potato Bread

Nutty Orange Loaf

1. Grease bottom and halfway up sides of a 9×5×3-inch baking pan; set aside. Shred 1 tablespoon peel from oranges; set aside. Section oranges, reserving 1½ cups sections. Store remaining sections for later use.

2. In a large bowl combine the all-purpose flour, whole wheat flour, wheat germ, baking soda, and salt; make a well in the center. Set aside.

3. In a blender container combine orange sections, banana, eggs, sugar, oil, and vanilla. Cover; blend until smooth. Pour into flour mixture; stir just until combined. Fold in nuts and orange peel. Turn into prepared pan. Bake in a 350° oven for 60 to 65 minutes or until a wooden toothpick inserted in center comes out clean. Cool on wire rack for 10 minutes. Remove from pan; cool. For easy slicing, wrap and store overnight. If desired, serve with Orange Butter.

Orange Butter: *In a small bowl combine ⅓ cup softened butter, 1 tablespoon sifted powdered sugar, and 1 teaspoon finely shredded orange peel.*

Nutty Orange Loaf

Wheat germ and whole wheat flour contribute earthy flavor tones and texture to this nut-studded, orange-infused quick bread.

Prep: 30 minutes Bake: 1 hour Oven: 350°F
Makes: 1 loaf (16 servings)

    5 to 6 oranges
 1¼ cups all-purpose flour
  ¾ cup whole wheat flour
  ⅓ cup toasted wheat germ
    1 teaspoon baking soda
  ¼ teaspoon salt
    1 small banana, cut up
    2 eggs
    1 cup sugar
  ⅓ cup cooking oil
    1 teaspoon vanilla
  ½ cup chopped pecans
       Orange Butter (optional)

Cheddar-Corn Rolls

Cornmeal makes its way into many breads of the Southwest, including tortillas and corn bread. Here the grain adds texture and color to old-fashioned yeasty dinner rolls.

Prep: 45 minutes Rise: 2¼ hours
Bake: 15 minutes Oven: 375°F
Makes: 18 rolls

    4 to 4½ cups all-purpose flour
  ¾ cup cornmeal
    2 packages active dry yeast
 1¼ cups buttermilk or sour milk*
  ¼ cup sugar
    3 tablespoons butter or cooking oil
    3 tablespoons Dijon-style mustard
    2 teaspoons salt
    2 eggs
    1 cup shredded sharp cheddar cheese

1. In a large mixing bowl combine 1½ cups of the flour, cornmeal, and yeast; set aside.

2. In a saucepan combine buttermilk, sugar, butter, mustard, and salt; heat and stir until mixture is lukewarm (120°F to 130°F). Add buttermilk mixture to flour mixture; add eggs and cheese. Beat with an electric mixer on low to medium speed for 30 seconds, scraping sides of bowl constantly. Beat for 3 minutes on high speed. Stir in as much of the remaining flour as you can with a wooden spoon.

3. On a lightly floured surface, knead in enough remaining flour to make a moderately stiff dough that is smooth and elastic (6 to 8 minutes). Place dough in greased bowl; turn to grease surface. Cover; let rise until double (about 1½ hours).

4. Punch dough down. Cover; let rest for 10 minutes. Divide into 18 equal portions. Shape each portion into a ball, pulling edges under to make a smooth top. Place balls 1 inch apart on greased baking sheets; press down each ball to slightly flatten. Cover and let rise in a warm place until nearly double (about 45 minutes). Bake in a 375° oven for 15 to 18 minutes or until rolls sound hollow when lightly tapped.

Note: To make sour milk, place 4 teaspoons lemon juice in a glass measuring cup. Add milk to equal 1¼ cups total. Stir; let stand for 5 minutes.

Make-Ahead Tip: *After shaping, refrigerate dough, covered, for 4 to 24 hours. Uncover; let stand at room temperature for 30 minutes before baking.*

Coconut-Pecan Sticky Rolls

Coconut, pecans, orange marmalade, and maple syrup come together in one amazing cinnamon roll. Have them ready with coffee for Christmas morning visitors.

Prep: 35 minutes Rise: 1½ hours
Bake: 12 minutes Cool: 15 minutes
Oven: 375°F Makes: 24 rolls

- 3 to 3½ cups unbleached all-purpose flour or all-purpose flour
- 1 package active dry yeast
- 1 cup milk
- ⅓ cup granulated sugar
- ⅓ cup unsalted butter
- ½ teaspoon salt
- ¾ cup shredded coconut
- ¾ cup chopped pecans
- ½ cup packed brown sugar
- 2 teaspoons ground cinnamon
- ¼ cup unsalted butter
- ¼ cup maple-flavored syrup
- ½ cup orange marmalade
- ½ cup unsalted butter, melted

1. In a large mixing bowl combine 1½ cups flour and yeast. In a medium saucepan heat and stir the milk, granulated sugar, the ⅓ cup butter, and salt until warm (120°F to 130°F) and butter almost melts; add to flour mixture. Beat with electric mixer on low speed for 30 seconds, scraping bowl. Beat on high speed for 3 minutes. Using a wooden spoon, stir in as much remaining flour as you can.

2. Turn out dough onto a lightly floured surface. Knead in enough of the remaining flour to make a moderately stiff dough that's smooth and elastic (6 to 8 minutes total). Shape dough into a ball. Place in lightly greased bowl; turn once to grease surface. Cover; let rise until double (about 1 hour). Punch down. Divide in half. Cover; let rest for 10 minutes.

3. Meanwhile, lightly grease 24 (2½-inch) muffin cups. In a small bowl combine coconut, pecans, brown sugar, and cinnamon; set aside. In a small saucepan heat the ¼ cup butter and syrup until butter is melted. Place 1 teaspoon of the syrup mixture in each muffin cup. Sprinkle with a rounded tablespoon of the coconut mixture.

4. Roll half the dough into a 12×8-inch rectangle. Thinly spread half the orange marmalade on dough. Roll up from a long side; seal seams. Cut into 12 slices. Repeat with remaining dough and orange marmalade. Place, cut side down, into each muffin cup. Drizzle tops evenly with the ½ cup melted butter. Cover; let rise until nearly double (about 30 minutes).

5. Bake in a 375° oven for 12 to 15 minutes or until golden brown. Cool slightly. Invert onto a serving plate. Spoon any nut mixture left in pans over rolls. Serve warm.

Fruit-and-Nut Ring

Plums and apricots grow abundantly in the groves of California's fertile orchards. When dried, the fruits work beautifully in many recipes, including this gorgeous coffee cake. Hint: To offer as a gift, place a small covered bowl of icing in the center and include instructions for drizzling the icing over the ring before serving. Pictured on page 59.

Prep: 30 minutes Rise: 45 minutes
Bake: 25 minutes Oven: 350°F
Makes: 1 ring (12 servings)

- 1 **16-ounce loaf frozen bread dough, thawed**
- ⅓ **cup granulated sugar**
- ⅓ **cup packed brown sugar**
- 3 **tablespoons all-purpose flour**
- ½ **teaspoon ground cinnamon**
- ¼ **cup butter**
- ½ **cup snipped dried plums (prunes)**
- ½ **cup snipped dried apricots**
- ¼ **cup chopped almonds, toasted (see note, page 131)**
- 1¼ **cups sifted powdered sugar**
- ¼ **teaspoon vanilla**
- ¼ **teaspoon almond extract**
- 1 **to 3 tablespoons milk**

1. Line a large baking sheet with foil; grease foil; set aside. On a lightly floured surface roll dough to a 15×9-inch rectangle.

2. In a medium bowl stir together granulated sugar, brown sugar, flour, and cinnamon. Using a pastry blender, cut in butter until the mixture resembles coarse crumbs. Stir in dried plums, dried apricots, and almonds. Sprinkle fruit mixture over dough. Roll up dough from a long side; seal seam. Place dough on prepared baking sheet. Bring ends together to form a circle; pinch seam to seal. Using kitchen scissors or a sharp knife, cut slits at 1-inch intervals around the ring. Gently turn each slice so one of the cut sides is down (see photo, page 59). Cover and let rise in a warm place until nearly double (45 to 60 minutes).

3. Bake in a 350° oven for 25 minutes or until ring sounds hollow when lightly tapped. Remove bread from foil; cool completely on a wire rack.

4. For icing, in a small bowl stir together powdered sugar, vanilla, almond extract, and enough of the milk to make an icing of drizzling consistency. Drizzle over ring before serving.

Wild Rice Rolls

Wild rice adds irresistible nuttiness to traditional dinner rolls. Hint: If you make these rolls ahead, reawaken their fresh-baked aroma by heating them just before serving. Wrap room-temperature rolls in foil and place in a 350° oven for 5 to 10 minutes, just until warm.

Prep: 1 hour 25 minutes Rise: 1¼ hours
Bake: 12 minutes Stand: 10 minutes
Oven: 375°F Makes: 24 rolls

- 3¾ to 4¼ **cups all-purpose flour**
- 2 **packages active dry yeast**
- 1 **tablespoon snipped fresh parsley or 1 teaspoon dried parsley, crushed**
- ¾ **cup cooked wild rice***
- 1¼ **cups water**
- 3 **tablespoons butter or margarine**
- 2 **tablespoons sugar**
- 1 **teaspoon instant chicken bouillon granules**
- ¾ **teaspoon salt**
- 2 **tablespoons milk**
  Butter or margarine, melted

1. In a large mixing bowl stir together 1½ cups of the flour, yeast, parsley, and wild rice; set aside.

2. In a medium saucepan stir together the water, the 3 tablespoons butter, sugar, bouillon granules, and salt. Heat and stir just until warm (120°F to 130°F), the butter almost melts, and the bouillon dissolves. Add water mixture to flour mixture. Beat with an electric mixer on low speed for

30 seconds, scraping sides of bowl. Beat on high speed for 3 minutes. Stir in as much of the remaining flour as you can with a wooden spoon.

3. Turn out dough onto a lightly floured surface. Knead in enough of the remaining flour to make a moderately stiff dough that is smooth and elastic (6 to 8 minutes total). Shape into a ball. Place in a lightly greased bowl; turn once to grease surface. Cover and let rise in a warm place until double (45 to 60 minutes).

4. Punch down dough. Turn out onto a lightly floured surface. Divide in half. Cover; let rest for 10 minutes. To shape rosette dinner rolls, roll each half of dough on a lightly floured surface into a 12×10-inch rectangle. Cut each rectangle crosswise into twelve 10×1-inch strips. Stretch each strip to form a 12-inch rope; tie in a loose knot, leaving 2 long ends. Tuck top end under roll, bring up bottom end, and tuck it into center of roll. Place on lightly greased baking sheets.

5. Cover and let rise in a warm place until almost double (30 minutes). Brush with milk. Bake in a 375° oven for 12 to 15 minutes or until golden. Remove from oven and brush tops with additional butter.

*To prepare ¾ cup cooked wild rice: *Rinse ¼ cup wild rice well. Simmer, covered, in 1 cup water about 40 minutes or until most of the water is absorbed. Drain any remaining water.*

Make-Ahead Tip: *Store baked rolls, wrapped in plastic wrap or foil, at room temperature up to 3 days. Or freeze baked rolls up to 2 months; thaw frozen rolls before warming.*

Wild Rice grows wild in the marshes of Minnesota, a state known as the "Land of 10,000 Lakes." Although it's called "rice"—presumably because it grows in water—it's actually a grain, the seeds of a marsh grass. Fans call it the "caviar of grains" and enjoy its nutty richness in dishes from pilafs and stuffings to soups, salads, and casseroles. It even adds a lovely flavor and texture to bread, as in Wild Rice Rolls, shown right. Uncooked wild rice keeps indefinitely when stored in a cool, dry place or in the refrigerator.

Wild Rice Rolls

Desserts of the Season

AUTUMN AND WINTER host a merry march of irresistible fruits, from Florida's bright citrus to Oregon's sweet, juicy pears. Fruits and nuts from orchards, brambles, and timbers star in many of these irresistible desserts; others feature favorite flavors from particular areas—sweet maple syrup from New England, espresso from the Pacific Northwest, a tipple of bourbon from the South. You'll find the perfect dessert for any occasion throughout the season. Whether you're looking for something as homespun as an apple slump or an all-out dazzler, the selections are as varied as the wonderful ingredients featured.

Orchard Pear Tart (recipe, page 82)

Maple-Apple Slump

Maple-Apple Slump

Slumps are in the same category as cobblers, crisps, grunts, and bettys—old-fashioned American desserts of baked fruit topped with yummy biscuit dough, pastry cutouts, bread, or streusel. The name comes from the way it slumps when spooned into a bowl.

Prep: 30 minutes Bake: 30 minutes
Oven: 350°F Makes: 12 servings

2	cups all-purpose flour
2	teaspoons baking powder
½	teaspoon baking soda
3	cups peeled, coarsely chopped cooking apples
1½	cups pure maple syrup
½	teaspoon ground cinnamon
¼	teaspoon ground nutmeg
1	cup chopped pecans, toasted (see note, page 131)
1	cup buttermilk or sour milk*
¼	cup butter, melted
	Ice cream or whipped cream

1. In a medium bowl combine flour, baking powder, baking soda, and ½ teaspoon *salt*; set mixture aside.

2. In a medium saucepan combine apples, maple syrup, cinnamon, and nutmeg. Bring to boiling; reduce heat. Simmer, covered, for 5 minutes or until apples are just tender. Remove from heat; stir in pecans. Pour into a greased 2-quart square baking dish.

3. For biscuit topping, add buttermilk and melted butter to flour mixture in bowl. Stir just until combined. Drop batter in 12 mounds onto apple mixture in baking dish. Bake in a 350° oven for 30 to 35 minutes or until a toothpick inserted into biscuit topping comes out clean. Serve warm with ice cream.

*Note: *To make 1 cup sour milk, place 1 tablespoon lemon juice or vinegar in a glass measuring cup. Add enough milk to equal 1 cup total; stir. Let mixture stand for 5 minutes before using.*

French Apple Cream Pie

Few senses transport you into the realm of home-baked goodness more thoroughly than the scent of an apple pie baking. A creamy, custardy mixture spooned into the piping hot crust gives this version of apple pie an irresistibly rich finish.

Prep: 30 minutes Bake: 50 minutes
Oven: 375°F Makes: 8 servings

	Pastry for Double-Crust Pie
¾	cup sugar
2	tablespoons all-purpose flour
1	teaspoon ground cinnamon
	Dash salt
	Dash ground nutmeg
6	cups peeled, thinly sliced cooking apples, such as Rome, Granny Smith, Golden Delicious, or Jonathan
2	beaten eggs
½	cup sugar
2	ounces cream cheese, cubed and softened (¼ of an 8-ounce package)
½	cup dairy sour cream
1	tablespoon lemon juice

1. Prepare pastry. On a lightly floured surface, slightly flatten 1 ball of pastry dough. Roll from center to edge into a 12-inch circle. Ease pastry into a 9-inch pie plate, being careful not to stretch; set aside.

2. In a large bowl combine the ¾ cup sugar, flour, cinnamon, salt, and nutmeg. Add apple slices to sugar mixture; gently toss to coat. Transfer apple mixture to the pastry-lined pie plate. Trim pastry to edge of pie plate.

3. Roll remaining pastry into a 12-inch circle; cut out and set aside five 1½-inch circles from the pastry. Place pastry on filling; trim ½ inch beyond edge of plate. Fold top pastry under bottom pastry. Crimp edge as desired.

4. Place pie on a 15×10×1-inch baking pan. To prevent overbrowning, cover edge of pie with foil. Bake in a 375° oven for 25 minutes. Remove foil. Bake for 25 to 30 minutes more or until bubbly.

5. Meanwhile, in a small saucepan combine eggs and the ½ cup sugar. Cook, stirring constantly, over medium heat until mixture just coats a metal spoon (about 10 minutes). Remove from heat; add cream cheese in small amounts, stirring until cream cheese is melted. Stir in sour cream and lemon juice.

6. Remove the pie from the oven. Immediately and carefully spoon cream mixture into the holes in piecrust top. Cool slightly. Serve warm.

Pastry for Double-Crust Pie: *In a bowl combine 3 cups all-purpose flour and ¾ teaspoon salt. Using a pastry blender, cut 1 cup of lard or shortening into the flour until pieces are the size of small peas. Using 7 to 8 tablespoons total of ice water, sprinkle 2 tablespoons of water over part of the flour mixture; stir gently with a fork. Push moistened dough to the side of the bowl. Repeat, using 1 tablespoon of water at a time, until all the flour mixture is moistened. Divide dough in half. Form each half into a ball. Makes enough pastry for one double-crust pie or two pastry shells.*

French Apple Cream Pie

Boston Cream Pie

Boston Cream Pie

Chefs speculate that Boston Cream Pie, created at Boston's Parker House Hotel in the mid-1850s, was originally called a pie because it lacked the height of typical cakes. Serve this beautiful from-scratch version as a stunning finale to any holiday dinner.

Prep: 40 minutes Bake: 35 minutes
Chill: 6 hours Oven: 350°F Makes: 12 servings

- 1⅓ cups milk
- 1 vanilla bean, split lengthwise, or 1 teaspoon vanilla
- ⅓ cup granulated sugar
- 2 tablespoons cornstarch
- 3 beaten egg yolks
- 2 tablespoons butter
- 2 eggs
- ¾ cup milk
- 2 cups sifted cake flour
- 2 teaspoons baking powder
- ¼ teaspoon salt
- ½ cup butter, softened
- 1 cup granulated sugar
- 1 teaspoon vanilla
- ¼ cup whipping cream
- 1 teaspoon instant coffee crystals
- 4 ounces semisweet chocolate, finely chopped
- 1 tablespoon light-color corn syrup
- ¼ cup sifted powdered sugar

1. For the filling, in a small saucepan combine 1 cup of the milk and the vanilla bean, if using. Heat over medium heat until bubbles appear at the edges; set aside. In a medium saucepan combine ⅓ cup granulated sugar and cornstarch.

Stir in remaining ⅓ cup milk. Remove vanilla bean from hot milk and scrape seeds into milk-cornstarch mixture in saucepan. Discard pod. Gradually add hot milk to milk-cornstarch mixture in saucepan. Cook and stir over medium heat until thickened and bubbly. Cook and stir for 2 minutes more. Gradually stir about 1 cup of the hot milk mixture into the beaten egg yolks, stirring constantly. Return all the mixture to the saucepan. Cook and stir until bubbly. Cook and stir for 2 minutes more. Remove from heat. Stir in the 2 tablespoons butter until melted. Stir in 1 teaspoon vanilla, if using.

2. For the cake, allow 2 eggs and the ¾ cup milk to stand at room temperature for 30 minutes. Grease and lightly flour a 9-inch springform pan; set aside. In a medium bowl stir together cake flour, baking powder, and salt; set aside.

3. In a large mixing bowl beat the ½ cup softened butter with an electric mixer on medium to high speed for 30 seconds. Add 1 cup granulated sugar and 1 teaspoon vanilla. Beat for 4 to 5 minutes until fluffy. Add eggs, 1 at a time, beating well after each addition. Alternately add flour mixture and the ¾ cup milk to butter mixture, beating on low speed after each addition just until combined. Spread batter into the prepared pan.

4. Bake in a 350° oven for 35 to 40 minutes, or until a wooden toothpick inserted near center comes out clean. Cool in pan on a wire rack for 10 minutes. Remove cake from pan; invert onto a wire rack. Remove pan bottom; invert cake again onto a wire rack. Cool thoroughly on rack.

5. For glaze, in a small saucepan combine whipping cream and coffee crystals. Bring to boiling; remove from heat. Stir in chocolate until mixture is smooth and chocolate is melted. Stir in corn syrup and powdered sugar until smooth. Let stand for 10 minutes to cool and thicken.

6. Split cake horizontally with a long serrated knife. Place bottom layer on serving plate. Spoon custard filling onto bottom layer; spread to ½ inch from edge. Top with remaining cake layer, cut side down. Spoon glaze onto center of cake. Spread evenly, letting some run down sides. Chill for 4 to 24 hours. Let stand at room temperature for 30 minutes before serving.

Maple Streusel Cake

A wave of buttery, nutty streusel nestles inside this delectably moist cake. It's a good potluck choice because it serves so many.

Prep: 50 minutes **Bake:** 50 minutes
Cool: 10 minutes **Oven:** 350°F
Makes: 16 servings

3	tablespoons all-purpose flour
3	tablespoons packed brown sugar
1½	teaspoons ground cinnamon
3	tablespoons butter
1	cup chopped walnuts or pecans
¾	cup butter, softened
1	cup granulated sugar
½	cup maple sugar or packed brown sugar
3	eggs
2½	cups unbleached all-purpose flour or all-purpose flour
½	cup whole wheat flour
1	tablespoon baking powder
1½	cups dairy sour cream
2	teaspoons vanilla
1	cup sifted powdered sugar
¼	cup pure maple syrup

1. Grease and flour a 10-inch fluted tube pan; set aside. For the streusel mixture, in a medium bowl stir together the 3 tablespoons flour, the 3 tablespoons brown sugar, and cinnamon. With a pastry blender cut in the 3 tablespoons butter until crumbly. Stir in ¾ cup of the nuts; set aside.

2. In a large mixing bowl beat the ¾ cup butter with an electric mixer on medium to high speed for 30 seconds. Beat in granulated sugar and the ½ cup maple sugar until combined. Add eggs, 1 at a time, beating well after each addition.

3. In a large bowl stir together the 2½ cups all-purpose flour, the whole wheat flour, and the baking powder. In a small bowl stir together the sour cream and vanilla. Add flour mixture and sour cream mixture alternately to butter mixture, beating on low speed after each addition just until combined. Spoon half of the batter into prepared pan. Sprinkle with streusel mixture. Spoon remaining batter over streusel mixture.

4. Bake in a 350° oven for 50 to 55 minutes or until a wooden toothpick inserted near center comes out clean. Cool in pan on a wire rack for 10 minutes; remove from pan.

5. Stir together powdered sugar and maple syrup; drizzle syrup mixture over warm or cooled cake. Sprinkle with remaining nuts. Serve warm or completely cooled.

Maple Streusel Cake

Maple Syrup For New Englanders, late February and early March is known as "sugaring season." That's when they tap maple trees for sap. Each tree yields about 10 gallons of sap, which is then boiled and boiled—and boiled—until all the water content is eliminated. The result is about a quart of the sweet golden-brown elixir known as maple syrup. When you purchase maple syrup, you may notice that the label carries a grade on it, such as Grade A Light Amber, Grade A Medium Amber, Grade A Dark Amber, and Grade B (these designations vary according to state). Which one is best? It depends on how strong you want your syrup to taste. In general, the higher the grade, the lighter the color and more delicate the flavor. As the grades lower, the syrup becomes darker in color and more maple in flavor. Purists say that any grade of real maple syrup tastes better than imitation syrups. Be sure to enjoy real maple syrup in the glaze for Maple Streusel Cake.

Best-Ever Bourbon Brownies

Bourbon Some people claim that bourbon is as American as apple pie—certainly it's an all-American product, different in taste and character than either Scotch or Irish whiskey. Made from at least 51 percent corn (for sweetness) and other grains, bourbon is aged in oak barrels that have been charred inside. This charring technique caramelizes the sugar in the wood, which imbues the spirit with distinct caramel color and flavor. Enjoy a splash of bourbon in such recipes as Best-Ever Bourbon Brownies.

Best-Ever Bourbon Brownies

Technically a brownie is a bar cookie, but this one is so rich and decadent—with a hint of bourbon—that it easily stands in for dessert. Hint: If you prefer the brownies without the bourbon, omit the drizzling step.

Prep: 30 minutes Bake: 20 minutes
Oven: 350°F Makes: 16 to 20 brownies

⅓	cup butter
½	cup granulated sugar
2	tablespoons water
1	cup semisweet chocolate pieces
2	eggs
1	teaspoon vanilla
¾	cup all-purpose flour
¼	teaspoon baking soda
¼	teaspoon salt
½	cup chopped pecans
2	to 3 tablespoons bourbon
3	tablespoons butter, softened
1½	cups sifted powdered sugar
2	to 3 teaspoons milk
¼	teaspoon vanilla
1	ounce semisweet chocolate, melted

1. Grease an 8×8×2-inch baking pan; set aside. In a medium saucepan, combine the ⅓ cup butter, the granulated sugar, and water. Cook and stir over medium heat just until boiling. Remove from heat. Add the 1 cup chocolate pieces; stir until chocolate is melted. Stir in eggs and vanilla, beating lightly with a spoon just until combined. Stir in flour, baking soda, and salt. Stir in pecans. Spread batter into prepared pan.

2. Bake in a 350° oven about 20 minutes or until edges are set and begin to pull away from sides of pan.

3. Using a fork, prick the warm brownies several times. Drizzle bourbon evenly over brownies; cool in pan on a wire rack.

4. For frosting, in a small mixing bowl beat the 3 tablespoons butter with an electric mixer on medium to high speed for 30 seconds. Gradually add powdered sugar, beating well. Slowly beat in 2 teaspoons of the milk and the vanilla. If necessary, beat in remaining milk to reach spreading consistency. Spread over brownies; drizzle melted chocolate over frosting.

Sweet Potato Pie with Eggnog and Brandy

Sweet potato pie is a favorite in the South, and this rich version dresses up the classic for the holidays with sweet eggnog and a touch of brandy.

Prep: 30 minutes Bake: 55 minutes
Cook: 35 minutes Oven: 400°F/350°F
Makes: 2 pies (10 servings each)

 | Pastry for Double-Crust Pie
3 | pounds sweet potatoes
2 | tablespoons granulated sugar
½ | teaspoon ground cinnamon
¼ | cup butter, melted
1½ | cups eggnog
2 | eggs
2 | tablespoons brandy
½ | cup granulated sugar
1 | cup packed brown sugar
1 | teaspoon ground cinnamon
1 | teaspoon vanilla
 | Whipped cream and cinnamon (optional)

1. In a large saucepan cook sweet potatoes, covered, in boiling lightly salted water for 35 to 40 minutes or until very tender; drain. Cool until easy to handle.

2. Meanwhile, roll each pastry half to 12-inch-diameter circles. Place each pastry sheet in a 9-inch pie plate. Trim pastry ½ inch beyond edge of pie plate. Fold under extra pastry; crimp and decorate edge as desired. Prick pastry with fork. Combine 2 tablespoons granulated sugar and ½ teaspoon ground cinnamon; sprinkle in pastry shells. Bake pastry in a 400° oven for 5 minutes. Carefully remove from oven to wire racks. Reduce oven temperature to 350°.

3. Peel sweet potatoes; place in an extra large mixing bowl; beat with an electric mixer until mashed. Beat in melted butter, eggnog, eggs, brandy, the ½ cup granulated sugar, brown sugar, the 1 teaspoon cinnamon, and vanilla; divide evenly between the pastry shells.

4. Bake for 50 minutes or until a knife inserted off-center comes out clean. Cool on wire rack; cover and chill to store. If desired, serve with whipped cream sprinkled with cinnamon.

Pastry for Double-Crust Pie: *In a medium bowl combine 2 cups all-purpose flour and ½ teaspoon salt. Using a pastry blender, cut in ⅔ cup shortening until pieces are the size of small peas. Using 6 to 7 tablespoons total cold water, sprinkle 1 tablespoon water over part of the flour mixture; gently toss with a fork; push to side of bowl. Repeat, adding 1 tablespoon of water at a time, until all flour mixture is moistened. Divide dough in half. Use immediately or cover and chill until needed.*

Sweet Potato Pie with Eggnog and Brandy

Luscious Orange Sponge Cake

Luscious Orange Sponge Cake

Decadent desserts are always popular, but sometimes after a heavy holiday meal guests crave something light and luscious. When that's the case, turn to this heavenly creation made with airy whipped cream slathered over and between layers of a springy sponge cake.

**Prep: 45 minutes Bake: 15 minutes
Chill: 4 hours Oven: 375°F Makes: 12 servings**

½	**cup all-purpose flour**
1	**teaspoon baking powder**
4	**egg yolks**
⅓	**cup granulated sugar**
1	**teaspoon finely shredded orange peel or ¾ teaspoon orange extract**
½	**cup orange juice**
4	**egg whites**
½	**cup granulated sugar**
	Sifted powdered sugar
	Orange Whipped Cream
3	**tablespoons orange liqueur or orange juice**
	Sliced kumquats, orange peel strips, and/or fresh mint (optional)

1. Lightly grease a 15×10×1-inch jelly roll pan. Line bottom with waxed paper; grease the paper; set aside. In a small bowl stir together the flour and baking powder; set aside.

2. In a medium mixing bowl beat egg yolks with an electric mixer on high speed for 4 to 5 minutes or until thick and lemon color. Gradually add the ⅓ cup granulated sugar, beating on high speed until sugar is almost dissolved. Stir in orange peel and orange juice. Thoroughly wash beaters. In another mixing bowl beat egg whites on medium speed until soft peaks form. Gradually add the ½ cup granulated sugar, beating until stiff peaks form. Fold egg yolk mixture into beaten egg whites. Sprinkle flour mixture over egg mixture; gently fold in until combined. Evenly spread batter in the prepared pan.

3. Bake in a 375° oven for 15 minutes or until cake springs back when lightly touched. Immediately loosen edges of cake from pan; turn out cake onto a towel sprinkled with sifted powdered sugar. Carefully peel off waxed paper. Transfer towel and cake to wire rack; cool. Prepare Orange Whipped Cream.

4. Cut cake crosswise into three 10×5-inch rectangles. Brush top of each rectangle with some of the liqueur. Place one cake rectangle on a platter. Top with 1 cup Orange Whipped Cream. Add another cake rectangle; top with another 1 cup of cream mixture. Add last cake layer. Frost top and sides of cake with remaining cream mixture. Cover; chill for 4 to 24 hours. If desired, garnish with kumquat slices, orange peel strips, and/or fresh mint.

Orange Whipped Cream: *In a medium saucepan combine 1¼ cups sugar, ½ cup all-purpose flour, and a dash of salt. In a bowl stir together 4 egg yolks, ½ teaspoon orange peel, ⅔ cup orange juice, and 2 tablespoons lemon juice. Whisk yolk mixture into sugar mixture in saucepan. Cook and stir over medium heat until thickened and bubbly. Reduce heat; cook and stir for 1 minute more. Remove from heat. (The mixture will be thick and will thicken more as it cools.) Set pan in a bowl of ice water; stir occasionally until cool.*

In chilled medium mixing bowl beat 2 cups whipping cream with chilled beaters of electric mixer on medium speed until stiff peaks form. Stir about ½ cup of whipped cream into orange mixture to lighten. Gently fold cooled orange mixture into remaining whipped cream. Use immediately.

Chocolate-Blackberry Torte

This high-and-mighty Southern-style cake is unforgettable, thanks to a mix of chocolate, berries, and bourbon. Pureed blackberries—frozen will do just fine—make it extra moist.

Prep: 30 minutes **Bake:** 35 minutes
Cool: 10 minutes **Oven:** 350°F
Makes: 12 servings

Nonstick cooking spray
2½ cups fresh blackberries or frozen
  blackberries, thawed
3 cups all-purpose flour
2 cups sugar
¾ cup unsweetened European-style
  cocoa powder
2 teaspoons baking soda
1 teaspoon salt
1 cup buttermilk or sour milk (see note,
  page 70)
⅔ cup cooking oil
2 tablespoons vinegar
2 teaspoons vanilla
1½ cups blackberry jam
  Bourbon Sweet Cream
  Fresh blackberries (optional)
  Mint sprigs (optional)

1. Coat two 9×2-inch round baking pans or two 9-inch springform pans with cooking spray. Line bottoms of pans with waxed paper or parchment; lightly coat paper with cooking spray; set aside. (If you have only 1 springform pan, bake half the batter at a time. Store the remaining batter, covered, in the refrigerator until ready to bake.)

2. In a blender container or food processor bowl place the 2½ cups blackberries. Cover and blend or process until smooth. Strain berries through a fine mesh sieve (you should have about 1 cup puree); discard seeds. Set puree aside.

3. In a large bowl stir together the flour, sugar, cocoa powder, baking soda, and salt. Make a well in the center of the flour mixture; set aside. In a medium bowl whisk together the berry puree, buttermilk, cooking oil, vinegar, and vanilla; stir just until moistened. Divide batter between the prepared pans.

4. Bake in a 350° oven about 35 minutes or until a wooden toothpick inserted near center comes out clean. Cool cakes in pans for 10 minutes. Remove from pans; remove waxed paper or parchment. Cool completely on wire racks.

5. To assemble, use a sharp knife to carefully slice each cake layer in half horizontally, making four layers. Place the first layer on a large serving plate. Spread ½ cup of the jam on the cake layer. Repeat with 2 cake layers and the remaining jam. Top with the remaining cake layer. Frost top and sides of cake with Bourbon Sweet Cream. Chill torte up to 2 hours before serving. If desired, garnish with fresh blackberries and mint sprigs.

Bourbon Sweet Cream: *In a chilled medium mixing bowl combine 2 cups whipping cream and ⅓ cup bourbon. Beat with chilled beaters of an electric mixer on medium speed until soft peaks form (tips curl). Add ½ cup sugar and beat until stiff peaks form (tips stand straight). Makes about 4 cups.*

Chocolate-Blackberry Torte

Wisconsin Cheese Pie

Wisconsin Cheese Pie

This pie is similar to cheesecake only lighter—a delightful finish to a holiday meal.

Prep: 40 minutes Bake: 35 minutes
Oven: 450°F/350°F Makes: 8 servings

> Pastry for Single-Crust Pie
> 1 lemon
> 1 8-ounce package cream cheese, cut up and softened
> 1 3-ounce package cream cheese, cut up and softened
> 1 cup sugar
> 1 cup cottage cheese or ricotta cheese
> 1 teaspoon vanilla
> 3 eggs, beaten
>   Lemon peel strips (optional)

1. Prepare pastry. On lightly floured surface, roll pastry to 12-inch circle. Wrap pastry around rolling pin. Unroll and ease pastry into 9-inch pie plate. Trim and crimp edges, if desired. Line pastry with a double thickness of foil. Bake in a 450° oven for 8 minutes. Remove foil. Bake for 4 to 5 minutes more or until set and dry. Set aside. Reduce oven temperature to 350°.

2. Using a fine shredder, remove yellow peel from lemon; set peel aside. Peel and cut-up lemon, removing the seeds; set aside.

3. In a food processor bowl or blender container combine the cream cheese, sugar, cottage cheese, vanilla, shredded lemon peel, and cut up lemon.

Cover and process or blend until smooth, stopping and pushing mixture down as needed.

4. In a large bowl place the beaten eggs. Using a wooden spoon, stir cheese mixture into eggs. Pour into baked pastry shell. Bake in a 350° oven for 35 to 40 minutes or until center appears nearly set when shaken.

5. Cool on a wire rack for 1 hour. Cover and chill at least 4 hours before serving. If desired, garnish with lemon peel strips.

Pastry for Single-Crust Pie: *In a large bowl combine 1¼ cups all-purpose flour and ¼ teaspoon salt. Using a pastry blender cut in ⅓ cup shortening until pieces are the size of peas. Using 4 to 5 tablespoons total of cold water, sprinkle 1 tablespoon cold water at a time over part of the flour mixture; gently toss with a fork. Push moistened dough to the side of the bowl. Repeat until all is moistened. Form dough into a ball.*

Chocolate-Cranberry Cheesecake

Cranberry and chocolate seem like an odd couple, but tangy cranberries bring out the best in sweet chocolate. Shown on the cover.

Prep: 40 minutes Bake: 50 minutes
Cool: 45 minutes Chill: 4 hours
Oven: 350°F Makes: 12 servings

> 1¼ cups jellied cranberry sauce
> ¼ cup semisweet chocolate pieces
> ¾ cup finely crushed graham cracker crumbs
> ¾ cup finely crushed gingersnap crumbs
> 3 tablespoons granulated sugar
> 2 tablespoons all-purpose flour
> 6 tablespoons butter, melted
> 2 8-ounce packages cream cheese or reduced-fat cream cheese (Neufchâtel), softened
> 1 cup sifted powdered sugar
> 2 eggs
> 1 teaspoon vanilla

1. In a small saucepan combine cranberry sauce and chocolate pieces; cook and stir over medium-low heat until melted. Remove from heat; set aside cranberry-chocolate mixture.

2. In a medium bowl combine crushed graham crackers, crushed gingersnaps, granulated sugar, and flour; stir in melted butter. Press into bottom and 1½ inches up the side of an 8-inch springform pan or 1¼ inches up the side of a 9-inch springform pan; set aside.

3. In a large mixing bowl beat cream cheese and powdered sugar with an electric mixer on medium speed until fluffy. Add eggs and vanilla; beat on low speed just until combined. Set aside 1 cup of the cream-cheese mixture.

4. Spread remaining cream-cheese mixture in the crust-lined pan. Drop large spoonfuls of the cranberry-chocolate mixture onto the cream-cheese mixture in pan. Drop large spoonfuls of reserved cream-cheese mixture over cranberry-chocolate mixture. Using a table knife, swirl gently to marble.

5. Place springform pan in a shallow baking pan. Bake in a 350° oven for 50 to 55 minutes for an 8-inch pan or 45 to 50 minutes for a 9-inch pan or until center appears nearly set when shaken. Cool in pan on rack for 15 minutes. Loosen crust from side of pan; cool 30 minutes. Remove side of pan; cool. Cover; chill at least 4 hours.

Nutty Raisin Cream Pie

Rich raisin-studded filling is reason enough to love this pie. Two Southern touches—coconut and pecans—make it special.

Prep: 35 minutes Bake: 17 minutes
Chill: 3 hours Oven: 450°F Makes: 10 servings

    Pastry for Single-Crust Pie, opposite
1   **to 1½ cups raisins**
½   **cup sugar**
4   **teaspoons cornstarch**
1½ **cups whipping cream**
2   **eggs, beaten**
2   **tablespoons butter**

1   **teaspoon vanilla**
½   **cup flaked coconut**
½   **cup chopped pecans or walnuts**

1. Prepare pastry. On lightly floured surface, roll pastry to 12-inch circle. Wrap pastry around rolling pin. Unroll and ease pastry into 9-inch pie plate. Trim ½ inch beyond edge of plate; fold under and crimp edge. Prick pastry shell with a fork. Place trimmings and pastry shell on a baking sheet. Bake in a 450° oven for 8 to 10 minutes, removing trimmings when browned. Bake pastry shell for 4 to 6 minutes longer or until crust is golden. Cool on wire rack.

2. In a heavy medium saucepan combine raisins and enough water to cover; heat to boiling. Remove from heat; let stand for 10 minutes. Drain well; set aside.

3. In the same saucepan combine sugar, cornstarch, and dash *salt*. Stir in cream and eggs. Cook and stir until mixture thickens and bubbles. Cook and stir for 1 minute more. Stir in butter, vanilla, and drained raisins. Transfer to baked pie shell. Crumble pastry pieces (⅓ to ½ cup); combine with coconut and nuts. Sprinkle over pie. Bake pie in a 450° oven for 5 to 8 minutes or until coconut is browned. Cool; cover and chill at least 3 hours before serving.

Nutty Raisin Cream Pie

Cranberry-Pear Pie

Cranberry-Pear Pie

This is a tasty way to use two of winter's best-loved fruits. A sprinkling of coarse sugar on the crust shimmers like glistening snow— a magical way to get everyone into the spirit of the season.

Prep: 35 minutes Bake: 55 minutes
Cook: 5 minutes Oven: 375°F
Makes: 8 servings

> **Pastry for Double-Crust Pie**
> 1 **cup granulated sugar**
> 2 **tablespoons quick-cooking tapioca**
> 5 **cups thinly sliced, peeled, and cored pears**
> 1½ **cups cranberries**
> 1 **tablespoon milk**
>   **Coarse sugar**

1. Prepare pastry. On a lightly floured surface roll out half of the pastry to a circle about 12 inches in diameter. Transfer pastry circle to a 9-inch pie plate; ease into pie plate. Cover remaining pastry; set aside.

2. In a large saucepan combine the granulated sugar and tapioca. Stir in pears and cranberries until coated; let stand about 15 minutes or until a syrup begins to form, stirring occasionally. Bring to boiling over high heat. Reduce heat. Simmer, covered, for 3 to 5 minutes or just until pears are softened and cranberries begin to pop, stirring occasionally.

3. Transfer cranberry-pear mixture to the pastry-lined pie plate. Trim pastry to edge of pie plate. On a lightly floured surface roll remaining pastry into a 12-inch circle. If desired, with a 1-inch holiday cookie cutter, cut shapes from center of pastry, reserving cutouts. (Cut slits in pastry if not using cookie cutter.) Place pastry on filling and seal. Crimp edge as desired.

4. Brush milk on pastry. Sprinkle with coarse sugar. Top with holiday cutouts, if using. Brush cutouts with milk. Place pie on baking sheet. To prevent overbrowning, cover the edge of the pie with foil.

5. Bake in a 375° oven for 25 minutes. Remove foil. Bake for 30 to 35 minutes more or until fruit is tender and filling is bubbly. Cool on a wire rack. Serve warm or at room temperature.

Pastry for Double-Crust Pie: *In a bowl stir together 2¼ cups all-purpose flour and ¾ teaspoon salt. Using a pastry blender cut in ⅔ cup shortening until pieces are the size of small peas. Using 7 to 9 tablespoons total of cold water, sprinkle 1 tablespoon of water over the flour mixture; toss with a fork. Push to side of bowl. Repeat until all is moistened. Divide dough in half. Use immediately or cover and chill until needed.*

Espresso Custard

Influenced by the famous coffeehouses of Seattle, this sophisticated custard is perfect for an intimate New Year's Eve dinner party.

Prep: 25 minutes Stand: 30 minutes
Bake: 33 minutes Cool: 35 minutes
Oven: 350°F Makes: 3 or 4 servings

- ½ **cup whipping cream**
- ½ **cup milk (reduced-fat or whole)**
- 2 **tablespoons sugar**
- 2 **tablespoons espresso beans, slightly crushed**
- ⅛ **teaspoon ground cinnamon**
- ½ **of a vanilla bean, split lengthwise or ½ teaspoon vanilla**
- 1 **teaspoon coffee liqueur (optional)**
- 3 **egg yolks, beaten**
- 2 **ounces semisweet chocolate**
     Sweetened Whipped Cream
     Sugar-Glazed Pecans

1. In a heavy saucepan stir together the cream, milk, sugar, espresso beans, cinnamon, and vanilla bean. Heat until small bubbles appear around edge of pan, stirring occasionally. Remove from heat; cover and let stand for 30 minutes.

2. Meanwhile, place three 5-ounce pot de crème cups or four 3-ounce ramekins or 6-ounce custard cups in an 8×8-inch baking pan; set aside.

3. In a large bowl stir espresso mixture and coffee liqueur (if desired) into egg yolks. Strain the mixture through a fine sieve; discard solids. Set aside the espresso-egg yolk mixture.

4. In a small heavy saucepan melt chocolate over low heat. Remove from heat and stir until smooth. Using a wire whisk, very gradually whisk egg yolk mixture into the melted chocolate until smooth. Pour into cups or ramekins in pan. Pour hottest tap water into the baking pan about halfway up sides of the cups or ramekins.

5. Bake in a 350° oven until custards are just set when gently shaken (allow 33 to 35 minutes for the pot de crème cups or 25 minutes for the ramekins or custard cups). Remove from pan and cool to room temperature on wire racks (about 35 minutes). Serve at once, topped with Sweetened Whipped Cream and sprinkled with some of the Sugar-Glazed Pecans.

Sugar-Glazed Pecans: *In a heavy medium skillet melt 1 tablespoon unsalted butter over medium heat. Stir in ⅔ cup chopped pecans; stir to coat nuts with butter. Add 3 tablespoons sugar to skillet. Cook, stirring frequently with a long-handled wooden spoon, for 3 to 4 minutes until the sugar melts and caramelizes and the pecans are toasted. Turn out onto a lightly greased foil-lined heatproof surface. Cool; break or chop pecan mixture into small pieces. Makes about 1 cup.*

Sweetened Whipped Cream: *In a small chilled bowl whisk ¼ cup whipping cream, 2 teaspoons sugar, and ¼ teaspoon vanilla until soft peaks form.*

Orchard Pear Tart

Pears often make their way into holiday gift baskets, and this golden, glistening tart offers a beautiful way to showcase them. Pictured on page 69.

Prep: 50 minutes Bake: 48 minutes
Cool: 25 minutes
Oven: 450°F/375°F Makes: 8 to 10 servings

  1½ cups all-purpose flour
   2 tablespoons sugar
  ½ cup cold butter
   1 slightly beaten egg
   2 to 3 tablespoons ice water
   6 tablespoons butter
   1 egg
   1 egg yolk
  ⅓ cup sugar
   3 tablespoons all-purpose flour
   3 or 4 firm, ripe pears, such as Bartlett
      or Bosc
   1 cup water
   2 tablespoons lemon juice
  ⅓ cup apricot preserves
   1 tablespoon pear liqueur (optional)
      Sifted powdered sugar (optional)

1. For crust, in a medium bowl stir together the 1½ cups flour and the 2 tablespoons sugar. Using a pastry blender, cut in the ½ cup butter until pieces are the size of peas. In a small bowl combine the 1 beaten egg and 1 tablespoon of the ice water. Gradually stir egg mixture into flour mixture with a fork. Add remaining ice water, 1 tablespoon at a time, tossing gently until all the dough is moistened. Form dough into a ball. (If necessary, cover and refrigerate 30 minutes or until easy to handle.) Roll pastry on a lightly floured surface to a 12-inch circle. Carefully transfer pastry to an 11-inch tart pan with removable bottom. Ease pastry into pan; trim edges even with rim of pan. Line pastry with a double thickness of foil. Bake pastry in a 450° oven for 8 minutes. Remove foil. Bake for 5 to 6 minutes more or just until pastry is golden. Remove from oven. Reduce oven temperature to 375°.

2. For custard filling, in a small saucepan heat the 6 tablespoons butter over medium heat until golden brown; cool for 5 minutes. In a medium bowl beat the 1 egg and egg yolk with a wire whisk until combined. Whisk in ⅓ cup sugar, then the 3 tablespoons flour. Whisk in melted butter with all the brown bits; set aside.

3. Halve, core, and peel pears. Dip pears into a mixture of 1 cup water and the lemon juice; drain on paper towels. Beginning about ½ inch from the narrow end of each pear, use a sharp thin-bladed knife to cut pears, leaving pear attached at the top, into ⅛-inch slices. Carefully transfer pears to partially baked pastry, with narrow ends toward center of tart, fanning slices slightly. Spoon custard filling around pears.

4. Bake in a 375° oven for 35 to 40 minutes or until custard is set. Cool on a wire rack for 20 minutes. In a small saucepan melt preserves; strain to remove pieces of fruit. If desired, stir in pear liqueur. Spoon or brush preserves mixture evenly over pears. If desired, sprinkle with powdered sugar before serving.

Poires Belle Hélène

This classic French dessert is as sublime as it is simple, and this beautiful (belle) presentation is a terrific way to serve the season's most luscious pears. The fruit absorbs the essence of the vanilla- and orange-infused poaching liquid.

Prep: 20 minutes Cook: 20 minutes
Cool: 2 hours Makes: 6 servings

   6 firm pears
      Lemon juice
   1 tablespoon finely shredded orange peel
  1½ cups orange juice
  1½ cups water
  ¾ cup sugar
   1 vanilla bean, split lengthwise
   3 cups vanilla bean ice cream
      Chocolate-Orange Sauce
   3 tablespoons sliced almonds, toasted
      (see note, page 131)

1. Peel, halve, and core the pears, leaving stems intact, if desired. Rub pears gently with lemon juice to prevent browning. Set aside.

2. In a 12-inch skillet with a lid, combine orange peel, orange juice, water, sugar, and vanilla bean. Bring to boiling, stirring until sugar dissolves. Gently place pear halves, cut sides down, in pan. Return to boiling and spoon some liquid over pears. Simmer, covered, on medium-low heat for 10 minutes. Turn pears over. Simmer, covered, for 10 minutes more or until pears are tender. Set pan aside and let pears cool, covered, in the syrup for 2 to 8 hours.

3. To serve, remove pears from liquid; discard liquid. Place two cooled pear halves in serving dish. Place 2 small scoops of ice cream in cored centers of pears. Drizzle Chocolate-Orange Sauce over top. Garnish with toasted sliced almonds.

Chocolate-Orange Sauce: *In a small heavy saucepan melt ¾ cup semisweet chocolate pieces and ¼ cup butter over low heat. Add ⅓ cup sugar; gradually stir in ⅔ cup evaporated milk. Bring to boiling; reduce heat. Boil gently, uncovered, over low heat for 8 minutes, stirring frequently. Remove from heat. Sir in 2 tablespoons orange liqueur, if desired. Cool slightly. Makes about 1½ cups.*

Pears Grown mostly in California and the Pacific Northwest, pears are a beloved fruit of the holiday season, making their rich, sweet mark on a variety of recipes, including the Poires Belle Hélène dessert and the Tossed Greens with Goat Cheese Phyllo Packets salad (recipe, page 132). They also add a light, fresh note to an appetizer spread and go especially well with blue and Brie cheeses. Good varieties to choose for recipes include Bartlett and Bosc; both hold their shapes well during cooking. However, you must plan ahead because sometimes pears need to ripen at home a few days before using. To ripen, place them in a small clean paper bag; loosely close the bag and store at room temperature. Ripe pears yield to gentle pressure. Once ripe, transfer to the refrigerator to retard further ripening.

Poires Belle Hélène

83

Cheese for Your Holiday Table

CHEESE LOVERS, take note: In the last decade a veritable cheese revolution has taken place in America, with farmsteads from New England to California producing one-of-a-kind treasures. Bring them to your holiday table, and they'll do you proud. Here you'll discover some wonderful finds, along with many ways to savor and share them throughout the season. Keep it simple and serve them au naturel with crackers, fruit, and bread at an easygoing open house. Or use them in recipes and watch your holiday cooking really take off!

Laura
Chenel's Chèvre

Major Farm's
Vermont Shepherd
Sheep's Milk Cheese

Point Reyes
Original Blue

Vella Dry Jack

Crowley Cheese

New American Cheeses

Serious cheese lovers formerly looked to Europe for cheeses with intriguing flavors and textures. But these days more and more American states are home to cheese makers who produce their own unique handcrafted treasures that rival the best in Europe. Here's an introduction to eight distinctive American cheeses used in the recipes in this chapter. Some are time-honored, having been made for over a century, while others are highly regarded newcomers. As a group, they represent a fine introduction to the great variety of cheeses available.

Pictured from the top:

• **Major Farm's Vermont Shepherd:** This aged sheep's milk cheese is Vermont's stunning answer to Ossau-Iraty, a famous French cheese from the Pyrenees. It has a smooth, creamy texture and a sweet, rich, earthy flavor.

• **Point Reyes Original Blue:** This classic-style blue cow's milk cheese is handcrafted on a family dairy farm in Point Reyes, California. The creamy, full-flavored cheese has garnered rave reviews since it appeared in 2000.

• **Vella Dry Jack:** Made from cow's milk, this is a Jack cheese that's been aged, resulting in a drier, firmer texture and an irresistibly rich, sweet, nutty flavor.

• **Crowley Cheese:** Made by the oldest cheese producer in the United States, this cheese is in the cheddar family. It is hailed for its deep flavors, creamy texture, and for the luscious way it melts in cooking.

• **Laura Chenel's Chèvre:** California cheese maker Laura Chenel helped spark the American cheese revolution back in 1981 when she first began producing her artisanal goat cheeses. These days Chenel's full-flavor aged chèvres compare favorably to their French counterparts.

Not Pictured:

• **Capriole Chèvre:** Capriole's award-winning goat cheeses are made by hand on a family farm in Indiana and are available fresh, ripened, and aged.

• **Vermont Cheddar Cheeses:** If you've never tried a handcrafted Vermont cheddar cheese, you're in for a delicious surprise. In general, they're richer, creamier, and have a fuller flavor than the usual commercial varieties. Two high-quality, highly regarded varieties are Cabot Cheddar and Shelburne Farms Cheddar.

Finding Great American Cheeses:

Look for these cheeses at specialty cheese shops or in the deli cases of well-stocked supermarkets. Also see the list of sources, page 156. Be sure to buy extra—they'll all taste great as hors d'oeuvres, as part of a cheese course (see page 93), or to accompany a glass of wine while sitting by the fire anytime during the season.

Spicy Double-Cheese Straws

These tasty twists partner white cheddar with Parmesan for unforgettable flavor.

Prep: 35 minutes Bake: 10 minutes
Oven: 400°F Makes: about 40 crackers

- 1 cup all-purpose flour
- ¼ teaspoon cayenne pepper
- ⅛ teaspoon salt
- 1 cup finely shredded Cabot white cheddar, Shelburne white cheddar, or white cheddar (4 ounces)
- ¼ cup butter
- 3 to 5 tablespoons cold water
- 1 beaten egg
- 2 tablespoons grated Parmesan cheese

1. In a large bowl combine flour, cayenne pepper, and salt. Using a pastry blender, cut in cheddar cheese and butter until pieces are the size of small peas. Sprinkle 1 tablespoon of the cold water over part of the mixture. Gently toss with a fork. Push to side of bowl. Repeat until all of the flour mixture is moistened. Shape dough into a ball.

2. On a lightly floured surface flatten dough with your hands. Roll out dough from center to edges forming a 10-inch square. Brush with beaten egg; sprinkle with Parmesan cheese. Cut dough into 5×½-inch strips. Place the strips ½ inch apart on a lightly greased baking sheet.

3. Bake in a 400° oven for 10 to 12 minutes or until golden brown. Cool straws on wire rack.

Asiago Cheese Dip

Although Asiago cheese originally hails from Italy, American cheese makers have perfected their own versions.

Prep: 15 minutes
Cook: 3 hours on low; 1½ hours on high
Makes: 7 cups (28 servings)

- 1 cup chicken broth or water
- 4 ounces dried tomatoes (not oil-pack)
- 4 8-ounce cartons dairy sour cream
- 1¼ cups mayonnaise
- ½ of an 8-ounce package cream cheese, cut up
- 1 cup sliced fresh mushrooms
- 1 cup thinly sliced green onions (about 8)
- 6 ounces shredded Asiago cheese (1½ cups)
  Thinly sliced green onions
  Baguette slices, toasted

1. In a medium saucepan bring the chicken broth to boiling. Remove from heat; add the dried tomatoes. Cover and let stand for 5 minutes. Drain, discard the liquid, and chop the tomatoes (about 1¼ cups).

2. Meanwhile, in a 3½- or 4-quart crockery cooker combine the sour cream, mayonnaise, cream cheese, mushrooms, the 1 cup green onions, and Asiago cheese. Stir in the chopped tomatoes. Cover and cook on low-heat setting for 3 to 4 hours or on high-heat setting for 1½ to 2 hours. Stir before serving; sprinkle with additional green onions. Keep warm on low-heat setting for 1 to 2 hours. Serve warm with toasted baguette slices.

Blue Cheese-Walnut Spread

Serve with sliced apples, pears, and crackers.

Prep: 15 minutes Stand: 30 minutes
Makes: about 2 cups

- ½ pound Maytag blue cheese, Point Reyes blue cheese, or blue cheese
- ½ cup unsalted butter
- ½ cup finely chopped toasted walnuts
  Finely chopped walnuts, toasted (optional)

1. Let cheese and butter stand at room temperature for 30 minutes. Cut cheese into small pieces. Slice butter. Add cheese and butter to a food processor. Cover and process until almost smooth, scraping down sides of bowl with a rubber spatula as needed. Stir in the ½ cup walnuts. Transfer to a small serving bowl. If desired, sprinkle spread with additional walnuts.

Blue Cheese-Onion Tart

Blue Cheese-Onion Tart

Try using Point Reyes or Maytag blue cheese in this recipe. Thinly slice and serve as a sit-down appetizer to a dinner party. A puff of salad tossed with a sprightly vinaigrette would make the perfect accompaniment.

Prep: 45 minutes Bake: 26 minutes
Cool: 15 minutes Oven: 450°F/375°F
Makes: 12 appetizers

- ½ **of a 15-ounce package folded refrigerated unbaked piecrust (1 crust)**
- 2 **tablespoons butter or margarine**
- 1 **tablespoon packed brown sugar**
- 1 **teaspoon vinegar**
- 2 **medium onions, quartered lengthwise and thinly sliced (about 1⅓ cups)**
- 4 **ounces blue or feta cheese, crumbled (1 cup)**
- 2 **eggs**
- ½ **teaspoon dried chervil or marjoram, crushed**
- ¼ **teaspoon ground black pepper**
- ⅓ **cup milk, half-and-half, or light cream**
- 3 **tablespoons dry white wine or chicken broth**
- 2 **tablespoons snipped fresh parsley**
- 1 **beaten egg yolk**
- 1 **teaspoon water**
  Green onion curls (optional)

1. On a lightly floured surface roll piecrust from center to edges, forming a circle about 12 inches in diameter. Ease pastry into a 9-inch tart pan with a removable bottom, pressing dough up into fluted sides of pan. Trim edges, reserving scraps. Do not prick pastry. Line pastry with a double thickness of foil. Bake in a 450° oven for 8 minutes. Remove foil. Bake for 4 minutes more or until crust is dry and set. Reduce oven temperature to 375°.

2. Meanwhile, for filling, in a medium skillet melt butter; stir in brown sugar and vinegar. Add onions. Cook, uncovered, over medium-low heat for 12 to 15 minutes or until onions are tender and lightly browned, stirring occasionally.

3. In a medium mixing bowl beat cheese, eggs, chervil, and pepper with an electric mixer on low speed until combined (cheese will be lumpy). Stir in onion mixture, milk, wine, and parsley. Ladle filling evenly into baked tart shell.

4. Bake tart in a 375° oven about 20 minutes or until a knife inserted near center comes out clean and pastry is golden. Cool 15 minutes in pan on a wire rack.

5. Meanwhile, roll out piecrust scraps to ⅛-inch thickness; cut into decorative shapes with small cutters. Place on ungreased baking sheet. Brush lightly with a mixture of egg yolk and 1 teaspoon water. Bake cutouts in a 375° oven for 6 to 7 minutes or until golden.

6. Carefully remove sides of tart pan. Decorate top with baked cutouts and, if desired, green onion curls. Cut tart into wedges. Serve warm.

Crowley Cheese Nachos

Crowley sharp cheese is known for its terrific meltability, so it's perfect for nachos! To make your own homemade version of chorizo, see recipe, page 55.

Prep: 30 minutes Bake: 12 minutes
Oven: 400°F Makes: 6 to 8 servings

- 6 **ounces uncooked chorizo or bulk pork sausage**
- 12 **ounces shrimp in shells, peeled, deveined, and chopped**

⅓ cup lime-cilantro or chipotle salsa

⅓ cup snipped fresh cilantro

2 cups shredded Crowley sharp cheese, Colby cheese, or Monterey Jack cheese (6 ounces)

¾ cup finely chopped red sweet pepper

1 avocado, halved, pitted, peeled, and chopped
   Tortilla chips
   Fresh lime wedges

1. In a medium skillet cook and stir sausage over medium heat until browned. Drain off fat. Wipe out skillet. Return sausage to skillet. Add shrimp to sausage in skillet. Cook and stir for 2 to 3 minutes or until shrimp are opaque. Stir in salsa and cilantro. Spoon sausage mixture into a 10-inch deep-dish pie plate; sprinkle with cheese.

2. Bake in a 400° oven for 12 to 15 minutes or until bubbly and cheese is melted. Top with sweet pepper and avocado. Serve with tortilla chips and fresh lime wedges.

Cheddar Moons

Many artisanal versions of cheddar cheese are white in color rather than orange. That's because they lack a natural dye called annatto, which gives the orange varieties their color. Try white cheddar in these flaky, rich pastries, which—thanks to frozen puff pastry—are impressive yet easy to make.

Prep: 45 minutes Bake: 12 minutes
Oven: 400°F Makes: 24 appetizers

1 3-ounce package cream cheese, softened

1 egg yolk

1 teaspoon white wine vinegar

1 teaspoon snipped fresh chives

2 ounces Cabot or Shelburne white cheddar or sharp white cheddar cheese, shredded (½ cup)

2 slices apple-smoked bacon, crisp-cooked, drained, and crumbled

1 tablespoon chopped, pine nuts toasted (see note, page 131)

1 17.3-ounce package (2 sheets) frozen puff pastry, thawed

1 egg

1 tablespoon water
   Poppy seeds and/or sesame seeds (optional)

1. For the filling, in a small bowl beat together the cream cheese, egg yolk, vinegar, and chives until nearly smooth. Stir in cheddar cheese, bacon, and pine nuts.

2. On a lightly floured surface, roll 1 pastry sheet into a 12-inch square. Using a 3-inch round cookie cutter, cut out 12 circles. Top each circle with a rounded 1 teaspoon filling. Combine the 1 egg and 1 tablespoon water. Brush pastry edges with egg mixture. Fold circles in half over filling, pressing edges to seal. Repeat with remaining pastry sheet and filling.

3. Brush tops of pastries with egg mixture and, if desired, sprinkle with seeds. Place pastries on ungreased baking sheets. Bake in a 400° oven for 12 to 15 minutes or until golden brown. Serve the pastries warm.

Cheddar Moons and
Crowley Cheese Nachos

Polenta Cheese Circles

Polenta Cheese Circles

*Start with refrigerated polenta, top with
Vella Dry Jack cheese, then add whatever
strikes your fancy. It's a knife-and-fork
appetizer worthy of your next dinner party.*

Prep: 20 minutes Broil: 10 minutes
Makes: 12 servings (2 slices each)

  2 **16-ounce packages refrigerated polenta,
each cut into 12 slices**
  1 **cup finely shredded Vella Dry Jack
cheese or Parmesan cheese**
Toppers:
    Sliced green onions
    Slivered, pitted kalamata olives
    Roasted red sweet pepper strips
    Flaked smoked salmon (lox-style)
    **Peeled, deveined shrimp cooked
in butter**
    Snipped fresh herbs
    **Sliced shiitake mushrooms cooked
in butter**
    Pitted, peeled avocado slices
    Grape tomato slices
    Caramelized onions

    **Marinated artichoke hearts, drained
and chopped**
    **Finely shredded Vella Dry Jack cheese
or Parmesan cheese**

1. On a baking sheet arrange polenta slices. Broil
polenta 4 inches from heat for 5 minutes. Turn
slices over using a spatula (slices may be soft).
Sprinkle with the 1 cup cheese. Broil for 5 to
6 minutes more or until cheese is melted and
golden. Top cheese circles with desired toppings.

Warm Goat Cheese Salad

*Warm goat cheese salad is one of France's
most famous, and now that America has
many fine producers of artisanal goat cheese,
it has become much loved here too.*

Prep: 20 minutes Broil: 2 minutes
Makes: 6 servings

  3 **ounces soft goat cheese (chèvre)**
  6 **¼-inch slices baguette-style French
bread, lightly toasted**

2 tablespoons ground walnuts
¼ cup olive oil
2 tablespoons finely chopped shallots
1 tablespoon champagne or white wine vinegar
1 teaspoon coarse-grain brown mustard
1 teaspoon Dijon-style mustard
½ teaspoon salt
8 cups mixed baby greens
6 slices apple-smoked bacon, crisp-cooked, drained, and crumbled
Freshly cracked black pepper

1. Spread chèvre evenly on toasted baguette slices. Sprinkle with ground walnuts. Place baguettes on a baking sheet; set aside.

2. For vinaigrette, in a screw-top jar combine oil, shallots, vinegar, mustards, and salt. Cover and shake well. In a large bowl combine greens and bacon pieces. Add vinaigrette; toss to coat. Divide greens among serving plates.

3. Broil baguette slices 4 inches from heat for 2 to 3 minutes or until cheese is bubbling and lightly browned. Place 1 baguette crouton on each salad. Top salads with black pepper. Serve immediately.

Sheep's Milk Cheese Antipasto Bowl

This recipe calls for Major Farm's Vermont Shepherd sheep's milk cheese, but you can use another variety of sheep's milk cheese (known as Brebis in French), such as Ossau-Iraty from the French Pyrenees or Manchego from Spain. It's an easy yet festive way to start off a party.

Prep: 35 minutes
Makes: 16 servings

8 ounces Major Farm's Vermont Shepherd sheep's milk cheese or Brebis, cut into bite-size cubes
8 ounces Italian sausage (sopressata, hard salami, mortadella), skinned, if necessary, and cut into bite-size cubes

1 cup mixed olives,* pitted if desired
1 cup pickled mushrooms,* drained
1 cup pickled pepperoncini peppers, drained
1 cup grape tomatoes
¼ cup snipped fresh basil
½ cup olive oil
¼ cup red wine vinegar
2 teaspoons Dijon-style mustard
½ teaspoon ground black pepper
¼ teaspoon salt

1. In a large serving bowl combine cheese, sausage, olives, mushrooms, peppers, tomatoes, and basil. In a small bowl whisk together oil, vinegar, mustard, black pepper, and salt. Add to cheese mixture in bowl and toss to coat. Serve with wooden picks.

*Note: *Look in the deli section of supermarkets for mixed olives and marinated mushrooms.*

Make-Ahead Tip: *Prepare as directed, except do not stir in fresh basil until serving and let the cheese and sausage mixture stand at room temperature for 30 minutes before serving. Chill up to 24 hours.*

Sheep's Milk Cheese
Antipasto Bowl

Artichoke-Chèvre Stuffed Chicken Breasts

Slice into a golden-roasted chicken breast and out oozes a sumptuous filling of goat cheese, prosciutto, artichoke hearts, and just the right seasonings. Impressive yet easy, this entrée makes the perfect dinner-party dish.

Prep: 45 minutes Bake: 40 minutes
Oven: 350°F Makes: 8 servings

- ¼ **cup olive oil**
- 2 **teaspoons dried thyme, crushed**
- ¼ **teaspoon crushed red pepper**
- 2 **6-ounce jars marinated artichoke hearts, drained and chopped**
- 4 **ounces prosciutto, cut into thin strips**
- 3 **cloves garlic, minced**
- 6 **ounces Laura Chenel's chèvre or Capriole chèvre or other creamy goat cheese**
- 8 **large chicken breast halves (8 to 10 ounces each)**
   Salt and ground black pepper

1. For filling, in a medium skillet heat 2 tablespoons of the oil over medium heat. Add thyme and red pepper; cook for 1 minute. Stir in artichokes, prosciutto, and minced garlic. Cook and stir for 4 minutes. Remove from heat; stir in chèvre until melted and well combined. Cool filling completely.

2. Cut a horizontal pocket into each breast half by cutting from 1 side almost to, but not through,

the other side. Stuff pockets with cooled filling. Use wooden picks to close pockets to keep in filling. Sprinkle with salt and black pepper.

3. In a large nonstick skillet heat the remaining 2 tablespoons oil over medium-high heat. Brown chicken breasts, a few at a time, in hot oil. Transfer chicken to a large baking dish. (Chicken breasts can be covered with plastic wrap and chilled up to 4 hours before cooking.) Bake in a 350° oven for 40 to 45 minutes or until no longer pink (170°F). Remove the wooden picks before serving.

Blue Baked Potatoes

Twice-baked potatoes take a gourmet turn with blue cheese rather than cheddar.

Prep: 25 minutes Bake: 1¼ hours + 20 minutes
Cool: 15 minutes Oven: 350°F
Makes: 6 servings

- 6 **6-ounce russet potatoes**
- 2 **tablespoons butter**
- 2 **cloves garlic, minced**
- ½ **cup dairy sour cream**
- 3 **ounces Maytag blue cheese, Point Reyes blue cheese, or blue cheese, crumbled**
- ⅛ **teaspoon cayenne pepper**
   Snipped fresh chives (optional)
   Crisp-cooked bacon, crumbled (optional)

1. Scrub potatoes; prick with a fork. Bake potatoes in a 350° oven for 1¼ to 1½ hours or until tender. Cool slightly. Cut a thin slice from top of potato; scoop out pulp into a large bowl.

2. In a small skillet cook and stir the butter and garlic for 1 to 2 minutes over medium heat. Add butter mixture to potato pulp. Add sour cream, blue cheese, ½ teaspoon *salt*, and cayenne. Stir and mash with a fork until well blended. Spoon mixture into potato skins. (At this point, potatoes can be covered and refrigerated in an airtight container up to 48 hours.)

3. Arrange potatoes in a 2-quart rectangular baking dish. Bake, uncovered, in a 350° oven for 20 minutes (35 minutes for chilled potatoes). If desired, garnish with chives and crumbled bacon.

Artichoke-Chèvre Stuffed Chicken Breasts

Star Great American Cheeses in Your Cheese Course Why not serve a cheese course at one of your holiday get-togethers? Traditionally served after the entrée but before dessert, the cheese course is a great way to treat guests to a variety of bold flavors and sumptuous textures, and it's sure to enliven the conversation.

To design a fascinating cheese course, follow the rule of threes: Three is the perfect number of cheeses to serve—enough to offer variety but not so much as to overwhelm. One way to make your selection is to simply choose one each of goat, cow, and sheep's milk cheeses. The selection above illustrates this concept, while tapping into an all-American theme; left to right are Laura Chenel's Chèvre, Point Reyes Original Blue, and Major Farm's Vermont Shepherd Sheep's Milk. Another way to go about it is to vary textures and flavors, serving a soft cheese, a firm cheese, and a blue cheese; the above selection taps into that concept too.

Though Americans often pair cheese with fruit, the plate above takes a tip from the French and serves the trio with delicate greens lightly tossed with a tart vinaigrette. The bright, fresh mini-salad provides a crisp counterpoint to the creamy, dense cheeses.

American Wines
for Your
Holiday Table

WHETHER YOU'RE HOSTING a big Christmas dinner that draws cousins from three states or a casual trim-the-tree soup supper with your favorite neighbors, American wines are a natural fit for your holiday fare. And if you feel you're "all thumbs" when it comes to choosing wine, take heart! We've made the task easy and enjoyable by giving you a selection of wines grouped by the season's occasions, taking into consideration the foods traditionally served. So come along and see just how simple it is to find a great wine to enhance the terrific food you'll be serving in the months ahead.

American Wines: Just as Colorado's peaches taste different from Georgia's, American wines taste different from those of other parts of the world.

Wines, especially American ones, are an ideal addition to any gathering because they bring new flavor dimensions to every menu. And like the American character itself, their contributions tend to be bold, with lots of fruit flavors and mouth-filling texture. They work well in a variety of situations, from coat-and-tie cocktail parties to casual dinners to movie nights on the couch with a bowl of popcorn.

That affable nature makes American wines great companions for American foods. It all stems from the fact that the wines are crafted by vintners who understand the way we eat and entertain. In fact, because many vintners cook and eat the same as we do, they have a good idea of what we're serving at holiday potlucks, dinners, brunches, and impromptu after-work gatherings—and they've developed wines that go wonderfully with these occasions.

With wineries now in almost every state, it's possible to get wine that's an even closer match to your favorite local flavors and cooking techniques.

The selections featured are from United States wineries that distribute to all 50 states. If your curiosity is piqued and you want to continue exploring American wines or find wines from wineries in your region, start at wine specialty stores and liquor stores. For more information on the wines in this story, refer to Sources, page 156.

A note on serving temperatures: The taste of red wines will benefit from 45 minutes to an hour in the fridge before serving; the whites can handle up to two hours. Don't worry about wines being too cold because the warmth from a room full of merrymakers quickly takes the chill off any glass.

Wines for the Season

Thanksgiving to Christmas Eve:

Food is the focus at Thanksgiving as well as many of the gatherings leading up to Christmas; and two wines stand out as ideal mates for the Yule table.

Wine made from the Riesling grape is full of great peachy aromas and flavors usually complemented by a tiny bit of sweetness; they're often a pretty good deal too. Try the Kendall-Jackson Vintner's Reserve Riesling, Bonny Doon Pacific Rim Riesling, and Chateau St. Michelle Johannisberg Riesling.

The other good choice for this time of year is the red version of Zinfandel (not the white, which has its own charms but is a better match with summertime foods). Zinfandel is spicy and jammy and ideal for dinners and parties. Some good reasonably priced bottles include Ravenswood Vintner's Blend Zinfandel, Buena Vista Winery Zinfandel, or Chateau Souverain's Dry Creek Valley Zinfandel.

Bonny Doon Pacific Rim Riesling

Christmas Eve and Christmas Day:

On these two occasions into which great food, high spirits, and bustling activity are packed, the simplest wine selection is best. Pick one red, one white, and everyone will find something to like.

The white: Chardonnay is beloved because it goes well with food and so many people enjoy it. Chardonnays bring rich buttery, oak, pear, and apple flavors to the table, which beautifully complement roasted meats and winter vegetables that usually find their way onto holiday menus. Look for Forest Glen Winery Chardonnay, Stone Cellars Chardonnay, or Hawk Crest Chardonnay. For a bargain, try Inglenook California Chardonnay.

The red: The softness and richness of Merlot go well with holiday favorites such as roasts, goose, and those big pans of scalloped potatoes that everyone devours. Try Blackstone Syrah, Canyon Road Winery California Merlot, and Trinchero Family Selection Merlot—all reasonably priced.

Blackstone Syrah

New Year's Eve:

Because the centerpiece of New Year's Eve celebrations usually features appetizers with such big flavors as smoked salmon, onion dips, and spicy nuts, the bubbly you serve can do with a little sweetness to round out the appetizer flavors. If buying more than one bottle, split your purchases between bottles labeled "brut," which are more tart and not at all sweet, and "extra dry," which are slightly sweet. The making of sparkling wines involves more labor than other wines, so sparkling wines tend to be somewhat more expensive; nevertheless, some great picks for under $25 are available.

Roederer Estate

Look for Roederer Estate, Chandon Riche Extra Dry (which has the added attraction of being a wee bit pink), Sofia Blanc de Blancs, Mumm Cuvée M, and for a budget pick, Korbel Brut or Korbel Extra Dry. If you prefer something without bubbles, try a wine made from the Chenin Blanc grape; they're usually a tiny bit sweet, which is balanced by mouthwatering flavors of slightly sour fruits like pineapple and citrus. Look for Snoqualmie Chenin Blanc or Dry Creek Vineyard's Dry Chenin Blanc.

Snoqualmie Chenin Blanc

New Year's Day:

Long lunches and early dinners are the order of the day—and that's when Sauvignon Blanc is ideal because these wines combine light lemony flavors, a zingy palate-clearing bite, and a lightness on the tongue that is so welcome after the heavyweights of the weeks before. Some easy-on-the-wallet choices include St. Supery Napa Valley Sauvignon Blanc, Barefoot Cellars California Sauvignon Blanc, Geyser Peak Winery California Sauvignon Blanc, and Robert Hall Paso Robles Sauvignon Blanc.

Splurge wines for that special someone:

These are not the wines to choose when you're having 20 people over, because some cost more than $40. Select some of these when you have serious wine-lovers on your list: Kendall-Jackson Grand Reserve Merlot, Gallo of Sonoma Barrelli Creek Vineyard Cabernet Sauvignon, Beringer Sbragia Limited Release Chardonnay, Cakebread Cellars Russian River Chardonnay, Rombauer Vineyards Carneros Chardonnay, Columbia Winery Red Willow Vineyard Syrah, and Toasted Head Russian River Valley Chardonnay.

Crowd-pleasers for everyone:

These wines are sold everywhere, and for good reason. Head to warehouse stores and buy them by the case when you expect a big gathering. Look for these good values, which are often on sale:

No-fail white wines include Meridian Santa Barbara County Chardonnay, Gallo of Sonoma California Chardonnay, and Kendall-Jackson Vintner's Reserve Chardonnay.

Even if you buy too many of these red wines, you'll like having them around for the winter: Robert Mondavi Private Selection Cabernet Sauvignon or Heron Cabernet Sauvignon.

Can't decide between red or white? Go with a rosé such as Robert Hall Paso Robles Rosé de Robles, Bonny Doon Vin Gris de Cigare, and Sanford Pinot Noir Vin Gris.

Gallo of Sonoma Barrelli Creek Vineyard Cabernet Sauvignon

Robert Hall Paso Robles Rosé de Robles

Cookies from All Over the Country

LOOKING FOR FRESH new ideas for your holiday cookie tray? Why not imbue good old thumbprint cookies with rich eggnog flavors or reinvent the famous Lady Baltimore Cake as a cute little sandwich cookie? You could infuse Christmas cutout cookies with a shower of lime flavor or drop cookies with sweet-tart grapefruit and cranberries. And you can't go wrong with a selection that features America's favorite flavor— chocolate. Throughout this chapter you'll find many ways in which fruits, nuts, and cherished regional flavors lend charm and good taste to this year's cookie recipes.

Chocolate Buttons (recipe, page 113)

Maple Butter Cookies

Elegant maple leaf shapes hint at delicate maple flavor. Order maple sugar through specialty baking catalogs.

Prep: 45 minutes Chill: 1 hour
Bake: 10 minutes per batch Oven: 350°F
Makes: about 5 dozen cookies

1¼ cups butter, softened
¾ cup granulated sugar
½ cup maple sugar or ½ cup packed brown sugar plus ¼ teaspoon maple flavoring
1 egg
2 teaspoons vanilla
3 cups all-purpose flour
1 egg white
1 tablespoon water
   Maple sugar or granulated sugar

1. In a large mixing bowl beat butter with an electric mixer on medium to high speed for 30 seconds. Add ¾ cup granulated sugar and ½ cup maple sugar, beating on medium speed until fluffy. Beat in 1 egg and the vanilla. At low speed, beat in as much flour as you can with the mixer. Stir in any remaining flour with a wooden spoon. Gather dough into a ball; divide into 4 equal portions. Roll each portion between 2 sheets of waxed paper to ⅛-inch thickness. Cover and chill for 1 hour or until easy to handle.

2. Meanwhile, stir together egg white and water.

3. Working with 1 portion of rolled dough at a time, cut out shapes with a 3-inch leaf-shape cookie cutter. Use a spatula to place cookies 1 inch apart on ungreased cookie sheets. Brush cookies with egg white mixture. Sprinkle lightly with maple sugar. Use a toothpick to make leaf veins in the cutouts. Bake in a 350° oven for 10 to 12 minutes or until edges are firm. Cool on wire racks.

To Store: *Place cookies in layers separated by waxed paper in an airtight container; cover. Store cookies at room temperature up to 3 days or freeze up to 3 months.*

Lady Baltimore Cookies

This lovely filled cookie is patterned after the famous Lady Baltimore Cake—a tall beauty made with tender cake layers filled with fruit and nuts, then slathered with fluffy frosting.

Prep: 1 hour Chill: 4 hours
Bake: 10 minutes per batch Oven: 375°F
Makes: about 16 sandwiches

½ cup butter, softened
½ cup shortening
2 cups all-purpose flour
¾ cup granulated sugar
⅓ cup milk
1½ teaspoons finely shredded lemon peel
1 teaspoon almond extract
   Granulated sugar
⅓ cup butter, softened
4 cups sifted powdered sugar
3 tablespoons milk
1 teaspoon vanilla
¼ cup chopped golden raisins
¼ cup chopped dried figs
¼ cup chopped pecans, toasted (see note, page 131)

Maple Butter Cookies

Lady Baltimore Cookies

3 tablespoons chopped red and/or green candied cherries
Granulated sugar (optional)

1. In a large mixing bowl beat the ½ cup softened butter and shortening with an electric mixer on medium to high speed for 30 seconds. Beat in half of the flour. Beat in the ¾ cup granulated sugar, ⅓ cup milk, lemon peel, and almond extract. Beat in remaining flour until combined. Cover and chill for 4 hours or until easy to handle.

2. Shape dough into 1¼- to 1½-inch balls. Place balls 3 inches apart on an ungreased cookie sheet. Flatten balls to about 2½-inch rounds using the bottom of a glass dipped in granulated sugar. Bake in a 375° oven about 10 minutes or until lightly brown around edges. Transfer cookies to wire racks to cool.

3. In a large mixing bowl beat the ⅓ cup softened butter until smooth. Gradually add 1 cup of the powdered sugar, beating until well combined. Beat in 3 tablespoons milk and the vanilla. Gradually beat in enough of the remaining powdered sugar to make a filling of spreading consistency. Stir in raisins, figs, pecans, and candied cherries.

4. For sandwich cookies, spread filling on the flat side of half of the cooled cookies. Top spread cookies with remaining cookies, flat sides together. If desired, sprinkle tops of sandwich cookies with granulated sugar.

To Store: *Cover and chill assembled cookies up to 1 day. Or place unfilled cookies in layers separated by waxed paper in an airtight container; cover. Store at room temperature up to 3 days or freeze for up to 3 months. Thaw frozen cookies; assemble as directed.*

Lime Zingers

Put some zip on the holiday cookie tray—lime makes these cookies a standout.

**Prep: 40 minutes Bake: 8 minutes per batch
Oven: 350°F Makes: about 72 cookies**

- 1 **cup butter, softened**
- ½ **cup granulated sugar**
- 2 **teaspoons finely shredded lime peel**
- ¼ **cup lime juice (about 2 limes)**
- 2 **teaspoons vanilla**
- 2¼ **cups all-purpose flour**
- ¾ **cup finely chopped Brazil nuts or hazelnuts (filberts)**
- ½ **of an 8-ounce package cream cheese, softened**
- 1 **cup sifted powdered sugar**
- 1 **tablespoon lemon juice or lime juice
   Green food coloring**

1. In a large mixing bowl beat butter with an electric mixer on medium speed for 30 seconds. Add granulated sugar. Beat until combined, scraping sides of bowl occasionally. Beat in lime peel, the ¼ cup lime juice, and 1 teaspoon of the vanilla until combined. Beat in as much flour as you can with the mixer; stir in remaining flour. Stir in nuts. Divide dough in half.

2. On a lightly floured surface, roll each half of the dough to ¼-inch thickness. Cut shapes using floured 1- or 2-inch cutters. Place 1 inch apart on ungreased cookie sheet.

3. Bake in a 350° oven for 8 to 10 minutes or until edges are lightly browned. Transfer cookies to a wire rack to cool.

4. For frosting, in a small mixing bowl beat cream cheese, powdered sugar, lemon juice, and the remaining 1 teaspoon vanilla with an electric mixer on medium speed until smooth. Tint as desired with food coloring. Frost cookies or use frosting to pipe designs on cookies. Let stand until dry.

To Store: *Place cookies in layers separated by waxed paper in an airtight container; cover. Store at room temperature up to 3 days. Or freeze unfrosted cookies up to 3 months. Thaw frozen cookies; frost.*

Grapefruit-Cranberry Drops

Grapefruits from Southern groves and cranberries from Northern bogs are combined in this one-of-a-kind cookie.

**Prep: 45 minutes Bake: 9 minutes per batch
Oven: 350°F Makes: about 3 dozen cookies**

- ½ **cup snipped dried cranberries or cherries**
- ½ **teaspoon finely shredded grapefruit peel**
- 3 **tablespoons grapefruit juice**
- 1 **tablespoon light-color corn syrup**
- ½ **cup butter, softened**
- ¾ **cup granulated sugar**
- ½ **teaspoon baking powder**
- 1 **egg**
- 1¾ **cups all-purpose flour**
- ½ **cup chopped pecans, toasted (see note, page 131)
   Grapefruit Icing**

1. In a small bowl combine cranberries, grapefruit peel, grapefruit juice, and corn syrup; let stand for 15 minutes.

2. In a large bowl beat butter with an electric mixer on medium to high speed for 30 seconds. Add sugar, baking powder, and ⅛ teaspoon *salt;* beat until light and fluffy. Beat in egg. Beat in as much of the flour as you can with the mixer. Stir in any remaining flour, the dried fruit mixture, and pecans. Drop by rounded teaspoons 2 inches apart on ungreased cookie sheets.

3. Bake in a 350° oven for 9 to 11 minutes or until edges are very lightly browned. Transfer cookies to wire racks to cool. Drizzle with Grapefruit Icing.

Grapefruit Icing: *Stir together 1 cup sifted powdered sugar, 1 tablespoon softened butter, and enough grapefruit juice (2 to 4 teaspoons) to make a drizzling consistency.*

To Store: *Place undrizzled cookies in layers separated by waxed paper in an airtight container; cover. Store at room temperature up to 3 days or freeze up to 3 months. Thaw frozen cookies; drizzle with grapefruit icing.*

Orange-Coconut Bars

Orange-Coconut Bars

Pecans, coconut, and orange—three favorite Southern flavors—team up for one luscious bar cookie.

Prep: 15 minutes **Bake:** 38 minutes
Oven: 350°F **Makes:** 32 triangles

½	**cup all-purpose flour**
¼	**cup granulated sugar**
¼	**cup butter**
½	**cup finely chopped pecans**
2	**eggs**
¾	**cup granulated sugar**
2	**tablespoons all-purpose flour**
1½	**teaspoons finely shredded orange peel**
3	**tablespoons orange juice**
¼	**teaspoon baking powder**
1	**cup coconut**

1. Line an 8×8×2-inch baking pan with foil; set aside. For crust, in a medium bowl stir together the ½ cup flour and the ¼ cup sugar. Using a pastry blender, cut in butter until mixture resembles coarse crumbs. Stir in pecans. Press flour mixture into the bottom of prepared pan. Bake in a 350° oven for 18 to 20 minutes or until golden.

2. Meanwhile, in a medium mixing bowl combine eggs, the ¾ cup sugar, the 2 tablespoons flour, orange peel, orange juice, and baking powder. Beat for 2 minutes with an electric mixer on medium speed until combined. Stir in coconut. Pour coconut mixture over baked crust.

3. Bake for 20 to 25 minutes more or until edges are light brown and center is set. Cool in pan on wire rack. Using a serrated knife, cut into 2-inch squares. Cut squares diagonally to form triangles. Store in refrigerator.

To Store: *Place cookies in layers separated by waxed paper in an airtight container; cover. Store in the refrigerator up to 3 days.*

Black Walnut Pinwheels

Nuts—or Not? Nuts grow from coast to coast in America, and many bakers love the richness and character they bring to holiday treats. What do you do when someone in your family is allergic to nuts (or simply doesn't care for them)? In some recipes you can omit them; in others, they're essential. In general, if the nuts are finely ground and make up a substantial part of the filling or dough, you can't omit them. If they're a starring ingredient, as in Black Walnut Pinwheels, they're essential to the recipe. However, if they're sprinkled in at the last step, as with many brownies and drop cookies, you can leave them out.

Black Walnut Pinwheels

Native to America, black walnuts have a richer, stronger flavor than English walnuts. The intense flavor of black walnut may be too much on its own, but when rolled in a sweet, buttery cookie, it's pure heaven.

Prep: 35 minutes Chill: 3 hours
Bake: 7 minutes per batch Cool: 2 minutes
Oven: 375°F Makes: about 3½ dozen cookies

- ½ cup shortening
- ½ cup packed brown sugar
- ¾ teaspoon baking soda
- ¼ teaspoon salt
- 1 egg

- 1¼ cups all-purpose flour
- ⅓ cup butter, melted
- ⅔ cup packed brown sugar
- ½ teaspoon black walnut flavoring (optional)
- 1 cup finely ground black walnuts

1. In a medium mixing bowl beat shortening with an electric mixer on medium to high speed for 30 seconds. Add the ½ cup brown sugar, baking soda, and salt; beat until combined, scraping sides of bowl occasionally. Beat in egg until combined. Beat in as much of the flour as you can with the mixer. Using a wooden spoon, stir in any remaining flour. If necessary, cover and chill dough for 1 to 2 hours or until easy to handle.

2. Meanwhile, in a small bowl combine melted butter, the ⅔ cup brown sugar, walnut flavoring (if desired), and walnuts.

3. On a lightly floured surface, roll dough to a 12-inch square. Spread walnut mixture evenly over dough; roll up into a spiral. Seal seams and ends. Wrap in plastic wrap. Chill in refrigerator at least 3 hours or until firm enough to slice.

4. Using a sharp knife, cut dough into ¼-inch slices. Place slices 2 inches apart on ungreased cookie sheets.

5. Bake in a 375° oven for 7 to 9 minutes or until edges are lightly browned. Cool on cookie sheets for 2 minutes. Transfer cookies to a wire rack; cool.

To Store: *Place cookies in layers separated by waxed paper in an airtight container; cover. Store at room temperature up to 3 days or freeze up to 3 months.*

Eggnog-Nut Thumbprints

Eggnog flavorings, rich walnuts, and luscious filling make this an irresistible version of the ever-favorite thumbprint cookie. Hint: Pipe in the filling just before you serve them so the cookies hold their shape.

Prep: 50 minutes Bake: 12 minutes per batch
Oven: 375°F Makes: about 40 cookies

- ¾ **cup butter, softened**
- ½ **cup sugar**
- ⅛ **teaspoon ground nutmeg**
- 2 **egg yolks**
- 1 **teaspoon vanilla**
- 1½ **cups all-purpose flour**
- 2 **slightly beaten egg whites**
- 1½ **cups finely chopped walnuts**
- **Rum Filling**
- **Ground nutmeg**

1. In a large mixing bowl beat butter with an electric mixer on medium to high speed for 30 seconds. Add sugar and the ⅛ teaspoon nutmeg. Beat until combined, scraping sides of bowl occasionally. Beat in egg yolks and vanilla until combined. Beat in as much of the flour as

you can with the mixer. Stir in any remaining flour. If necessary, cover and chill dough about 1 hour or until easy to handle.

2. Shape dough into 1-inch balls. Roll balls in beaten egg whites; roll in chopped walnuts to coat. Place balls about 1 inch apart on greased cookie sheet(s). Press your thumb into the center of each ball.

3. Bake in a 375° oven for 12 to 15 minutes or until edges are lightly browned. Transfer cookies to a wire rack to cool. Just before serving, pipe or spoon about ½ teaspoon Rum Filling into the center of each cookie. Sprinkle with additional nutmeg.

Rum Filling: *In a medium mixing bowl beat ¼ cup butter, softened, with an electric mixer for 30 seconds. Beat in 1 cup sifted powdered sugar until fluffy. Beat in 1 teaspoon rum or ¼ teaspoon rum extract and enough milk (1 to 2 teaspoons) to make a spreading consistency.*

To Store: *Place cookies in layers separated by waxed paper in an airtight container; cover. Store unfilled cookies at room temperature up to 3 days (fill just before serving) or freeze unfilled cookies up to 3 months. Thaw cookies; fill just before serving.*

Eggnog-Nut Thumbprints

Sour Cream Sugar Cookies

No Christmas cookbook is complete without a recipe for classic sugar cookie cutouts. The sour cream adds dairyland richness to an already wholesome treat. Pictured on the cover and on page 110.

Prep: 40 minutes Chill: 1 hour
Bake: 7 minutes per batch Oven: 375°F
Makes: about 2 dozen cookies

- ½   cup butter, softened
- 1   cup sugar
- 1   teaspoon baking powder
- ¼   teaspoon baking soda
-     Dash salt
- ½   cup dairy sour cream
- 1   egg
- 1   teaspoon vanilla
- 1   teaspoon finely shredded lemon peel
- 2½ cups all-purpose flour
-     Meringue Powder Icing
-     Coarse sugar, edible glitter, and/or small multicolor decorative candies (optional)

1. In a large mixing bowl beat butter with an electric mixer on medium speed for 30 seconds. Add sugar, baking powder, baking soda, and salt. Beat until combined, scraping sides of bowl occasionally. Beat in sour cream, egg, vanilla, and lemon peel until combined. Beat in as much of the flour as you can with the mixer. Stir in any remaining flour with a wooden spoon. Divide dough in half. Cover and chill dough for 1 to 2 hours or until easy to handle.

2. On a well-floured surface, roll half of the dough at a time to ⅛- to ¼-inch thickness. Use floured cookie cutters to cut shapes; place shapes 1 inch apart on an ungreased cookie sheet.

3. Bake in a 375° oven for 7 to 8 minutes or until edges are firm and bottoms are very light brown. Transfer cookies to a wire rack to cool. Frost cookies with Meringue Powder Icing or use icing to pipe designs on cookies. If desired, decorate with coarse sugar, edible glitter, and/or small multicolor decorative candies.

Meringue Powder Icing: *In a medium mixing bowl beat together ¼ cup water and 2 tablespoons meringue powder until combined. Beat in 2¾ cups sifted powdered sugar to make a smooth, spreadable icing. If desired, tint some or all of the icing with paste food coloring.*

To Store: *Place cookies in layers separated by waxed paper in an airtight container; cover. Store at room temperature up to 3 days. Or freeze uniced cookies up to 3 months. Thaw frozen cookies; ice.*

Dried Cherry Deluxe Cookies

Late June and early July usher in cherry season, and it's a short season indeed. Fortunately dried cherries make it possible to enjoy the fruit any time of year. Cherries taste especially good in baked goods and pair beautifully with white chocolate and nuts.

Prep: 30 minutes Bake: 8 minutes per batch
Oven: 375°F Makes: about 4 dozen cookies

- 1   cup butter, softened
- 1   cup packed brown sugar
- 2   eggs
- 1   teaspoon baking soda
- ½   teaspoon salt
- 1½ cups all-purpose flour
- 2   cups dried tart cherries
- 1½ cups quick-cooking rolled oats
- ⅔   cup chopped pecans
- ⅔   cup white baking pieces

1. In a large bowl beat butter with an electric mixer on medium to high speed for 30 seconds. Add brown sugar, eggs, baking soda, and salt. Beat until combined, scraping sides of bowl occasionally. Beat in flour. Stir in cherries, oats, nuts, and baking pieces.

2. Drop dough by rounded teaspoons 2 inches apart onto an ungreased cookie sheet. Bake in a 375° oven for 8 to 9 minutes or until edges are lightly browned. Transfer cookies to a wire rack to cool completely.

To Store: *Place cookies in layers separated by waxed paper in an airtight container; cover. Store at room temperature up to 3 days or freeze up to 3 months.*

Fruit and Nut
Cheesecake
Bars

Fruit and Nut Cheesecake Bars

The irresistible ingredients of traditional Italian cheesecake—cherries, almonds, golden raisins, and ricotta cheese—get reinvented as an American bar cookie!

Prep: 20 minutes Bake: 25 minutes
Cool: 1 hour Chill: 2 hours Oven: 350°F
Makes: 20 bars

½   **cup butter**
1¼ **cups finely crushed graham crackers**
     (about 18)
1   **15-ounce container fat-free ricotta**
     cheese
1   **egg**
¼   **cup sugar**
2   **tablespoons all-purpose flour**
2   **teaspoons finely shredded orange peel**
1   **teaspoon almond extract**
½   **cup sliced almonds or chopped**
     hazelnuts (filberts)
⅓   **cup chopped candied cherries**
⅓   **cup golden raisins**

1. Place butter in a 9×9×2-inch baking pan. Place the pan in a 350° oven for 6 minutes or until butter is melted. Remove from oven. Stir crushed crackers into melted butter. Using a wooden spoon, press the crumb mixture firmly and evenly into the bottom of the pan. Set aside.

2. In a blender container or food processor bowl combine the ricotta cheese, egg, sugar, flour, orange peel, and almond extract. Cover and blend or process until smooth. Carefully spread cheese mixture over crumb mixture. Combine the almonds, cherries, and raisins; sprinkle over cheese layer.

3. Bake in a 350° oven for 25 to 30 minutes more or until edges are puffed and golden. Cool in pan on a wire rack for 1 hour; cover and chill for 2 hours. Cut into bars.

To Store: *Store the cooled bars, covered, in the refrigerator up to 3 days.*

Seattle Latte Brownies

Ever since coffee went gourmet in the '90s, it has found its way into multitudes of recipes. The coffee crystals in this recipe intensify the brownie's chocolate flavor.

Prep: 15 minutes Bake: 30 minutes
Oven: 350°F Makes: 16 brownies

6	ounces unsweetened chocolate (6 squares)
¾	cup butter
¼	cup water
1	tablespoon instant coffee crystals
1	cup granulated sugar
1	cup packed brown sugar
3	eggs
1	teaspoon vanilla
1¼	cups all-purpose flour
½	cup ground almonds
¼	teaspoon ground cinnamon
⅛	teaspoon salt
2	tablespoons sifted powdered sugar (optional)
¼	teaspoon unsweetened cocoa powder (optional)

1. Line a 9×9×2-inch baking pan with foil, grease well, and set aside.

2. In a large microwave-safe bowl place the chocolate, butter, water, and instant coffee crystals. Microwave on 100-percent power (high) for 2 to 4 minutes or until butter is melted, stirring once or twice. Remove from microwave oven; stir until chocolate is completely melted.

3. Transfer chocolate mixture to a large mixing bowl. Beat in granulated sugar and brown sugar with an electric mixer on low to medium speed until well combined. Add eggs and vanilla; beat at medium speed for 2 minutes. Add flour, almonds, cinnamon, and salt; beat at low speed until combined. Spread in prepared pan.

4. Bake in a 350° oven for 30 to 35 minutes or until a toothpick inserted in center comes out with fudgy crumbs. (Do not overbake.) Cool in pan.

5. Lift foil from pan. Cut brownies in squares. If desired, stir together the powdered sugar and cocoa powder. Sift or sprinkle on brownies.

To Store: *Place in layers separated by waxed paper in an airtight container; cover. Store at room temperature up to 1 week or freeze up to 3 months.*

Stuffed Date Drops

Stuff chewy dates with rich pecans, then pack them into a buttery cookie. Is it any surprise the results are fabulous? The Browned Butter Icing adds a touch of refinement.

Prep: 35 minutes Cook: 8 minutes per batch
Oven: 375°F Makes: 60 cookies

1¼	cups all-purpose flour
½	teaspoon baking powder
½	teaspoon baking soda
¼	teaspoon salt
1	pound pitted dates
60	to 70 pecan halves
¼	cup butter, softened
¾	cup packed brown sugar
1	egg
½	cup dairy sour cream
	Browned Butter Icing

1. In a small bowl stir together flour, baking powder, baking soda, and salt; set aside. Stuff each date with a pecan half; set aside.

2. In a medium mixing bowl beat butter with an electric mixer on medium to high speed

30 seconds. Add brown sugar; beat until combined, scraping sides of bowl occasionally. Beat in egg until combined. Alternately add flour mixture and sour cream to egg mixture, beating well after each addition. Gently stir in stuffed dates with a wooden spoon.

3. Drop dough by rounded teaspoons onto an ungreased cookie sheet, allowing 1 date per cookie. Bake in a 375° oven 8 to 10 minutes or until edges are lightly browned. Transfer to wire racks to cool. Drizzle Browned Butter Icing on cookies; let icing dry.

Browned Butter Icing: *In a small heavy saucepan heat ½ cup butter over medium heat until golden brown, stirring occasionally. Remove from heat; stir in 3 cups sifted powdered sugar and 1 teaspoon vanilla. Stir in enough water (2 to 3 tablespoons) to make a drizzling consistency.*

To Store: *Place cookies in layers separated by waxed paper in an airtight container; cover. Store at room temperature up to 3 days or freeze uniced cookies up to 3 months. Thaw frozen cookies; ice.*

Orange and Macadamia Nut Cookies

A cup of cornstarch may sound like a lot, but the result is buttery, nut-studded delights that melt in your mouth.

**Prep: 45 minutes Bake: 12 minutes per batch
Oven: 350°F Makes: 72 cookies**

- 4 **cups all-purpose flour**
- 2 **cups sifted powdered sugar**
- 1 **cup cornstarch**
- 2 **cups butter**
- 1 **cup chopped macadamia nuts or walnuts, toasted (see note, page 131)**
- 2 **egg yolks**
- 1 **tablespoon finely shredded orange peel**
- ⅓ **to ½ cup orange juice
  Granulated sugar
  Orange Frosting
  Finely chopped macadamia
  nuts (optional)**

1. In a large bowl combine flour, powdered sugar, and cornstarch. Using a pastry blender, cut in butter until mixture resembles coarse crumbs. Stir in the 1 cup nuts. In a small bowl combine egg yolks, orange peel, and ⅓ cup of the orange juice; add to flour mixture, stirring until moistened. If necessary, add enough of the remaining orange juice to moisten.

2. On a lightly floured surface knead dough until it forms a ball. Shape dough into 1¼-inch balls. Arrange balls on an ungreased cookie sheet. Dip bottom of a fluted glass in granulated sugar and use it to flatten each ball to ¼-inch thickness.

3. Bake in a 350° oven for 12 to 15 minutes or until edges begin to brown. Transfer to a wire rack; cool. Frost with Orange Frosting. If desired, sprinkle with finely chopped macadamia nuts.

Orange Frosting: *In a bowl combine 4 cups sifted powdered sugar, ⅓ cup softened butter, 2 teaspoons finely shredded orange peel, and enough orange juice (4 to 6 tablespoons) to make a spreading consistency.*

To Store: *Place cookies in layers separated by waxed paper in an airtight container; cover. Store at room temperature up to 3 days or freeze unfrosted cookies up to 3 months. Thaw frozen cookies; frost and, if desired, sprinkle with nuts.*

**Orange and Macadamia
Nut Cookies**

Chocolate is a combination of cocoa butter, chocolate liquor (the pressed liquid from roasted cocoa beans), and sugar. Although chocolate is one of America's favorite flavors, cocoa beans are not grown in North America—Hawaii is the only state that grows the tropical plant.

Here are a few ins and outs of cooking with this wildly popular ingredient:

• When a recipe calls for chocolate, use the real product, not imitation chocolate. Imitations substitute vegetable fat for the cocoa butter, and the difference in taste is obvious.

• Store chocolate well wrapped in a cool (55°F to 65°F) place; it will keep up to 1 year.

• If the chocolate develops a grayish haze on its surface, don't throw it away! Although the gray color (known as "bloom") looks unappetizing, it disappears when heated and will not affect the outcome of your recipes. The bloom appears when chocolate is stored in conditions that are too humid or warm.

• Feel free to interchange semisweet and bittersweet chocolate.

• If a recipe specifically calls for white chocolate, use a product that is clearly labeled as such. Other similar-sounding products, such as white baking bars, white baking pieces, white candy coating, and white confectionery bars, don't contain cocoa butter and are not true white chocolate.

Sour Cream Sugar Cookies (recipe page 106) and Chocolate Cookie Cutouts

Chocolate Cookie Cutouts

Chocolate lovers will be thrilled with this cookie. It takes one of the season's most beloved cookies—the Christmasy cutout— and imbues it with their favorite ingredient.

Prep: 50 minutes Chill: 1 hour
Bake: 8 minutes per batch Oven: 375°F
Makes: 2½ dozen cookies

½	cup butter, softened
1	3-ounce package cream cheese, softened
1½	cups sifted powdered sugar
¼	cup unsweetened cocoa powder
½	teaspoon baking powder
¼	teaspoon ground cinnamon
1	egg
½	teaspoon vanilla
1½	cups all-purpose flour
2	cups sifted powdered sugar
2	tablespoons milk
	Milk
	Paste food coloring
	Coarse sugar, edible glitter, and/or small multicolored decorative candies (optional)

1. In a medium mixing bowl beat butter and cream cheese with an electric mixer on medium speed for 30 seconds. Add the 1½ cups powdered sugar, cocoa powder, baking powder, and cinnamon; beat until combined. Beat in egg and vanilla. Beat in as much flour as you can with the mixer; stir in remaining flour with a wooden spoon. Divide dough in half. Cover and chill for 1 hour or until easy to handle.

2. On a lightly floured surface, roll each portion of dough to about ¼-inch thickness. Cut out with 2½- to 3-inch cookie cutters. Arrange cutouts 1 inch apart on an ungreased cookie sheet.

3. Bake in a 375° oven for 8 to 9 minutes or until edges are firm. Cool on cookie sheet for 1 minute. Transfer to wire racks to cool completely.

4. For the icing, stir together the 2 cups sifted powdered sugar and 2 tablespoons milk. Add additional milk, 1 teaspoon at a time, until the icing reaches piping consistency. Tint icing as desired. Use a decorating bag fitted with a fine writing tip to decorate cookies with icing. If desired, sprinkle with coarse sugar, edible glitter, and or multicolored decorative candies.

To Store: *Place cookies in layers separated by waxed paper in an airtight container; cover. Store at room temperature up to 3 days or freeze undecorated cookies up to 3 months. Thaw frozen cookies; outline with icing.*

Chocolate-Cinnamon Meringues

Meringue cookies add a light touch to a holiday cookie tray. Adding cinnamon and chocolate sets these apart.

Prep: 30 minutes Bake: 1¼ hours
Stand: 1½ hours Oven: 225°F
Makes: about 3½ dozen cookies

2 egg whites
½ teaspoon vanilla
¼ teaspoon cream of tartar
⅛ teaspoon salt
½ cup sugar
3 tablespoons unsweetened cocoa powder
⅛ teaspoon ground cinnamon
3 ounces semisweet chocolate, chopped

1. Allow egg whites to stand at room temperature for 30 minutes. Cover 2 large cookie sheets with parchment paper or foil; set aside.

2. In a large mixing bowl combine egg whites, vanilla, cream of tartar, and salt. Beat with an electric mixer on medium speed until soft peaks form (tips curl). Gradually add sugar, 1 tablespoon at a time, beating about 4 minutes on high speed until stiff peaks form (tips stand straight) and sugar is almost dissolved. Gently fold in cocoa powder and cinnamon.

3. Transfer meringue to a large pastry bag fitted with a large basket-weave tip (1D). Pipe meringue in 3-inch lengths onto prepared cookie sheets. Bake in a 225° oven for 1¼ hours. Turn off oven; let meringues dry in oven, with door closed, for 1½ hours. Remove from oven; cool completely on cookie sheets.

4. Remove meringues from paper or foil. In a small saucepan melt chocolate over low heat, stirring constantly. Remove from heat. Dip an end of each meringue into melted chocolate to a depth of 1 inch; shake off excess. Lay meringues on waxed paper; let stand until the chocolate is set. Store in an airtight container.

To Store: *Place cookies in layers separated by waxed paper in an airtight container; cover. Store at room temperature up to 3 days.*

**Chocolate and Sherry
Cream Bars**

Chocolate and Sherry Cream Bars

Not a fan of sherry? Customize your gourmet bars with kirsch, clear crème de cacao, orange liqueur, or another flavored clear liqueur. Whatever flavor you choose, the results will be dreamy.

**Prep: 25 minutes Bake: 25 minutes
Chill: 1¾ hours Oven: 350°F Makes: 60 bars**

1	cup butter
4	ounces unsweetened chocolate
4	lightly beaten eggs
2	cups granulated sugar
1	teaspoon vanilla
1	cup all-purpose flour
4	cups sifted powdered sugar
½	cup butter, softened
¼	cup half-and-half or light cream
¼	cup sherry
1	cup chopped walnuts (optional)
½	cup semisweet chocolate pieces
2	tablespoons butter
4	teaspoons sherry or water

1. For crust, in a large saucepan melt the 1 cup butter and unsweetened chocolate over low heat. Remove from heat. Stir in eggs, granulated sugar, and vanilla; lightly beat just until combined. Stir in flour. Spread chocolate mixture in a greased 15×10×1-inch baking pan. Bake in a 350° oven for 25 minutes. Cool. (Crust will be moist.)

2. For filling, in a large mixing bowl combine powdered sugar and the ½ cup softened butter. Beat with an electric mixer on low speed until combined. Gradually add half-and-half and the ¼ cup sherry; beat well. If desired, stir in nuts. Spread filling over crust; chill until firm.

3. For topping, in a small saucepan melt chocolate pieces and 2 tablespoons butter over low heat; remove from heat. Stir in the 4 teaspoons sherry until smooth. Drizzle topping over chilled filling. Chill slightly until set but not firm. With a knife, score top to outline bars; chill until firm. Cut into bars.

To Store: *Place bars in layers separated by waxed paper in an airtight container; cover. Store in refrigerator up to 3 days.*

112

Chocolate Buttons

In the world of mega-size cookies, these old-fashioned, cute-as-a-button gems work their charm on a cookie tray. Pictured on page 99.

Prep: 25 minutes Bake: 4 minutes per batch
Cool: 1 minute Oven: 375°F
Makes: about 12 dozen cookies

- ¼ cup butter, softened
- ½ cup packed dark brown sugar
- ¼ cup unsweetened cocoa powder
- 1 tablespoon milk
- 1 teaspoon vanilla
- ¼ teaspoon baking soda
- ⅔ cup all-purpose flour
- 4 ounces bittersweet chocolate
- 1½ teaspoons shortening
- ½ teaspoon mint extract

1. In a large mixing bowl beat butter, brown sugar, cocoa powder, milk, and vanilla with an electric mixer on medium speed until combined, scraping sides of bowl occasionally. Beat in baking soda and as much of the flour as you can with the mixer. Stir in any remaining flour with a wooden spoon. Divide dough in half.

2. On a lightly floured surface, roll half of the dough at a time to ¹⁄₁₆-inch thickness. Using floured 1- to 1½-inch round cookie cutters, cut out dough. Place cutouts 1 inch apart on an ungreased cookie sheet.

3. Bake in a 375° oven for 4 to 5 minutes or until edges are firm. Cool on cookie sheet for 1 minute. Transfer cookies to a wire rack and let cool.

4. In a small heavy saucepan melt chocolate and shortening over low heat, stirring constantly. Remove from heat; stir in mint extract. Cool. Spoon melted chocolate mixture into a small self-sealing plastic bag; snip off a tiny corner of bag. Drizzle chocolate on cookies. Let stand until set.

To Store: *Place undrizzled cookies in layers separated by waxed paper in an airtight container; cover. Store at room temperature up to 3 days or freeze up to 3 months. Thaw frozen cookies; drizzle with chocolate.*

Chocolate Clouds

These heavenly clouds are crackly on the outside and moist and chewy inside. The windfall of assorted nuts is irresistible.

Prep: 50 minutes Chill: 1 hour
Bake: 12 minutes per batch Oven: 350°F
Makes: about 5½ dozen cookies

- 4 eggs
- 3½ cups all-purpose flour
- 2 teaspoons baking powder
- 1 cup butter
- 4 ounces unsweetened chocolate, chopped
- 3 cups sugar
- 1 teaspoon vanilla
- 1 teaspoon almond extract
- 2 cups chopped assorted nuts (walnuts, pecans, and sliced almonds)
- 1 bag (6 ounces) semisweet chocolate pieces

1. Allow eggs to stand at room temperature for 30 minutes. Meanwhile, in a medium bowl combine flour and baking powder; set aside.

2. In a small saucepan combine the butter and chocolate. Cook and stir over medium-low heat until chocolate is melted. Transfer to an extra large mixing bowl; add sugar and beat on medium-high speed for 1 minute until combined. Add eggs, 1 at a time, beating well after each addition. Beat in vanilla and almond extract. Reduce speed to low and beat in as much of the flour mixture as you can. With a wooden spoon stir in nuts, chocolate pieces, and any remaining flour mixture. Cover and chill for 1 hour or until easy to handle.

3. Roll dough into 1¼-inch balls. Arrange balls 1½ inches apart on ungreased cookie sheets. Bake in a 350° oven for 12 minutes or until tops are cracked. Cool on wire racks.

To Store: *Place cookies in layers separated by waxed paper in an airtight container; cover. Store at room temperature up to 3 days or freeze up to 3 months.*

Chocolate Chunk Cookies

If you have serious chocolate lovers on your list of holiday cookie recipients, be sure to put these gems in their baskets. The triple hit of chocolate is an extra-indulgent treat that they'll long remember.

Prep: 30 minutes Bake: 9 minutes per batch
Oven: 375°F Makes: about 45 cookies

- 2 ounces unsweetened chocolate, chopped
- 1 cup butter, softened
- ¾ cup granulated sugar
- ¾ cup packed brown sugar
- 1 teaspoon baking soda
- 2 eggs
- 1 teaspoon vanilla
- 2 cups all-purpose flour
- 6 ounces white baking bar, cut into chunks
- 6 ounces semisweet or bittersweet chocolate, cut into chunks
- 1 cup chopped walnuts or pecans (optional)

1. Place unsweetened chocolate in a small heavy saucepan. Cook and stir over very low heat until chocolate is melted. Set aside to cool.

2. In a large mixing bowl beat butter with an electric mixer on medium to high speed for 30 seconds. Add the cooled chocolate, granulated sugar, brown sugar, and baking soda. Beat until combined, scraping sides of bowl. Beat in eggs and vanilla until combined. Gradually beat in flour. Stir in the white baking bar, semisweet chocolate chunks, and, if desired, nuts.

3. Drop by rounded tablespoons 3 inches apart on an ungreased cookie sheet. Bake in a 375° oven for 9 to 11 minutes or until edges are firm. Cool on a cookie sheet for 1 minute. Transfer cookies to a wire rack to cool.

To Store: *Place cookies in layers separated by waxed paper in an airtight container; cover. Freeze up to 1 month.*

Chocolate-Pistachio Wreaths

Is it possible to make a beautifully shaped cookie without a cookie cutter or a rolling pin? Simply shape and twist your way to these very merry wreaths. If you like, roll the light-color ropes in red colored sugar before twisting with the chocolate ropes.

Prep: 1¼ hours Chill: 30 minutes
Bake: 8 minutes per batch Oven: 375°F
Makes: about 22 cookies

- ¾ cup butter, softened
- ¾ cup sugar
- ¼ teaspoon baking powder
- 1 egg
- 1 teaspoon vanilla
- 1¾ cups all-purpose flour
- ¼ cup finely chopped pistachio nuts
- ¼ to ½ teaspoon almond extract (optional)
- 3 tablespoons unsweetened cocoa powder
- 2 tablespoons milk
- Berry Icing (optional)

1. In a large mixing bowl beat butter with an electric mixer on medium to high speed for 30 seconds. Add sugar and baking powder. Beat until combined, scraping sides of bowl occasionally. Beat in egg and vanilla until combined. Beat in as much of the flour as you can with the mixer. Stir in any remaining flour.

2. Divide dough in half. In a medium bowl combine half of the dough with pistachio nuts and, if desired, almond extract. Set aside. In another medium bowl combine remaining half of dough with cocoa powder and milk. Cover and chill both portions of dough for 30 to 60 minutes or until easy to handle.

3. On a lightly floured surface, shape each dough portion into a 12-inch log. Cut ½-inch slices from each log. Roll each slice into a 7-inch rope. Place a light and a dark rope side by side; twist together 5 or 6 times. Shape twists into a circle and gently pinch ends together. Place wreaths 2 inches apart on an ungreased cookie sheet.

4. Bake in a 375° oven about 8 minutes or until edges are just firm. Transfer cookies to a wire rack to cool. If desired, pipe clusters of berries on wreaths with Berry Icing; let icing dry.

Berry Icing: *In a small bowl stir together ½ cup sifted powdered sugar and 1 to 2 teaspoons milk to piping consistency. Stir in red paste food coloring.*

To Store: *Place cookies in layers separated by waxed paper in an airtight container; cover. Store at room temperature up to 3 days. Freeze undecorated cookies up to 3 months. Thaw frozen cookies; decorate.*

Chocolate-Covered Cherry Cookies

Everyone who sees this cookie will rightly assume that it's a rich, fudgy winner. Delight grows with the first bite—thanks to the sweet maraschino cherry surprise inside. Two tips for success: Use real chocolate, not imitation, and use sweetened condensed milk, not evaporated. Otherwise, the frosting will not bake properly.

Prep: 40 minutes Bake: 10 minutes per batch
Oven: 350°F Makes: about 4 dozen cookies

  1½ cups all-purpose flour
  ½ cup unsweetened cocoa powder
  ½ cup butter, softened
  1 cup sugar
  ¼ teaspoon salt
  ¼ teaspoon baking powder
  ¼ teaspoon baking soda
  1 large egg
  1½ teaspoons vanilla
  1 10-ounce jar maraschino cherries
  1 cup semisweet chocolate pieces
  ½ cup sweetened condensed milk

1. In a small bowl combine flour and cocoa powder; set aside. In a large mixing bowl beat the butter with an electric mixer on medium to high speed about 30 seconds. Add sugar, salt, baking powder, and baking soda; beat until well combined. Beat in egg and vanilla. Beat in as much of the flour mixture as you can with the mixer. Use a wooden spoon to stir in any remaining flour mixture.

2. Shape dough into 1-inch balls; place on ungreased baking sheets. Use your thumb to press down the center of each ball. Drain maraschino cherries, reserving juice. Cut large cherries in half. Place a whole cherry or half cherry in the center of each cookie.

3. In a small saucepan combine the chocolate pieces and sweetened condensed milk; cook and stir over low heat until chocolate is melted. Remove from heat. Stir in 4 teaspoons of the reserved cherry juice. Spoon about 1 teaspoon of the frosting over each cherry, spreading to cover cherry (frosting may be thinned with additional cherry juice, if necessary).

4. Bake in a 350° oven about 10 minutes or until edges are just firm. Transfer cookies to wire rack to cool.

To Store: *Place cookies in layers separated by waxed paper in an airtight container; cover. Store at room temperature up to 2 days or freeze up to 3 months.*

From top:
**Chocolate-Covered
Cherry Cookies
Chocolate-
Pistachio Wreaths**

A
Bountiful
Harvest
of Gifts

THIS YEAR GIVE the gifts that money can't buy: food gifts made with the hands that truly touch the heart. Choose Spinach, Arugula, and Orange Pesto or Fresh Mozzarella with Basil for the gourmet food lovers on your list, or Sweet Cherry Jam, Honey-Pear Preserves, or Ol' South Pralines for the more traditional crowd. Gingerberry Relish or Sweet Potato-Banana Butter will brighten any winter table. You're sure to find something for everyone on your list because the ideas in this chapter are as varied as the orchards, fields, and woodlands from which the ingredients spring.

Poinsettia-Shape Fruit Bread (recipe, page 127)

Honey-Macadamia Nut Fudge

Hawaii is the largest exporter of macadamia nuts, though California grows them as well. The buttery-rich nut works its magic on this divine fudge.

Prep: 20 minutes Cook: 25 minutes
Cool: 40 minutes Makes: 36 pieces

Butter
1½ cups granulated sugar
  1 cup packed brown sugar
  ⅓ cup half-and-half or light cream
  ⅓ cup milk
  2 tablespoons honey
  2 tablespoons butter
  1 teaspoon vanilla
  ½ cup coarsely chopped macadamia nuts, hazelnuts (filberts), or pecans
 36 Chocolate-Dipped Nuts (macadamia, hazelnuts [filberts], pecan halves, or additional chopped nuts) (optional)

1. Line an 8×8×2-inch baking pan with foil, extending foil over edges of the pan. Butter the foil; set aside.

2. Butter the sides of a heavy 2-quart saucepan.* In the saucepan combine granulated sugar, brown sugar, half-and-half, milk, and honey. Cook over medium-high heat until mixture boils, stirring constantly with a wooden spoon to dissolve sugars (about 8 minutes). Avoid splashing mixture on the sides of the pan. Carefully clip a candy thermometer to the side of the saucepan.

3. Cook sugar mixture over medium-low heat, stirring frequently, until thermometer registers 236°F, soft-ball stage (15 to 20 minutes). Mixture should boil at a moderate, steady rate over the entire surface. Remove saucepan from heat. Add the butter and vanilla; do not stir. Cool, without stirring, to lukewarm (110°F), 40 to 50 minutes.

4. Remove candy thermometer from saucepan. Beat vigorously with the wooden spoon until fudge just begins to thicken. Add coarsely chopped nuts. Continue beating until mixture is very thick and just starts to lose its gloss (about 10 minutes total).

5. Quickly turn fudge into the prepared pan. While fudge is warm, score it into 1¼-inch squares. When fudge is firm, use foil to lift it out of the pan; cut into squares. If desired, top fudge with Chocolate-Dipped Nuts or additional nuts. Tightly cover fudge; store in a cool, dry place.

***Note:** If your saucepan has a very wide diameter, cooking times will be shorter.*

Chocolate-Dipped Nuts: *In a small saucepan melt ½ cup semisweet chocolate pieces and 1 teaspoon shortening over low heat. Add 36 whole macadamia nuts, hazelnuts, or pecan halves. Stir to coat. Remove each with a fork, allowing excess chocolate to drip off. Place on a baking sheet lined with waxed paper. Allow to stand until set. Makes 36.*

Candy-Coated Cereal Drops

Say good morning, good afternoon, or good evening with these drop candies made with cereal, nuts, marshmallows, and a candy coating that keeps it all together.

Start to Finish: 30 minutes Stand: 1 hour
Makes: about 60 pieces

1½ cups tiny marshmallows
1½ cups sweetened puffed corn oat cereal with peanut butter or puffed corn cereal
1½ cups crisp rice cereal
1½ cups mixed nuts
1¼ pounds vanilla-flavor candy coating, cut up

1. Line 2 baking sheets with waxed paper; set aside. In a large bowl combine marshmallows, peanut butter cereal, rice cereal, and nuts; set cereal mixture aside.

2. In a 2-quart heavy saucepan melt candy coating over low heat, stirring constantly until smooth. Remove from heat; pour over cereal mixture. Stir gently to coat. Drop by rounded teaspoons onto prepared baking sheets. Let stand about 1 hour or until set. Store tightly covered up to 3 days.

-Ol' South Pralines

Ol' South Pralines

Here's an old Southern candy that's made more interesting with a splash of whiskey.

Prep: 25 minutes Cook: 20 minutes
Makes: about 36 pieces

  2 **cups sugar**
  1 **cup buttermilk or sour milk***
  1 **teaspoon baking soda**
 ⅛ **teaspoon salt**
2½ **cups pecan halves**
  2 **tablespoons butter**
 ¼ **cup whiskey**
  1 **teaspoon vanilla**

1. Line 2 large baking sheets with foil. Lightly grease foil; set aside.

2. In a heavy 3-quart saucepan combine sugar, buttermilk, baking soda, and salt. Cook and stir over medium heat until mixture comes to boiling, stirring constantly. Reduce heat to medium. Clip candy thermometer to side of pan.

3. Stir in pecans and butter; cook and stir until thermometer registers 234°F (about 20 minutes). Watch carefully and reduce heat, if necessary, to prevent mixture from boiling over. Remove from heat. Stir in whiskey and vanilla. Immediately beat the mixture vigorously with a wooden spoon about 7 minutes or until mixture begins to thicken. Quickly drop candy by spoonfuls onto prepared baking sheets. Store, covered, at room temperature up to 3 days.

*Note: *To make 1 cup sour milk, place 1 tablespoon lemon juice or vinegar in a glass measuring cup. Add enough milk to equal 1 cup total; stir. Let mixture stand for 5 minutes before using.*

Fresh Mozzarella
With Basil

Fresh mozzarella, loved for its soft texture and incredibly mild, sweet flavor, was once a hard-to-find delicacy, available in the United States only in Italian enclaves in major cities or as an Italian import at specialty food shops. These days it's more widely available across the country because producers responded to the growing appreciation for this fine cheese. Keep in mind that fresh mozzarella differs greatly from regular mozzarella—that semisoft, stretchy cheese that Americans have sprinkled on pizza and tucked into lasagna for decades. Regular mozzarella melts beautifully; fresh mozzarella does not. Therefore, fresh mozzarella is best served simply, as in Fresh Mozzarella with Basil.

Fresh Mozzarella with Basil

Present this with baguette bread or a box of gourmet crackers for a ready-to-savor gift.

Prep: 10 minutes Stand: 15 minutes
Chill: Up to 3 days Makes: 16 servings

- 16 **ounces fresh mozzarella cheese**
- ¼ **cup olive oil**
- 2 **tablespoons snipped fresh basil or 1 teaspoon dried basil, crushed**
- 1 **tablespoon dried whole mixed peppercorns, cracked**

1. Cut mozzarella into 1-inch pieces; place in a medium bowl. Stir in oil, basil, and cracked peppercorns. Cover and refrigerate up to 3 days. Let stand at room temperature for 15 minutes before serving.

Note: *To present as shown, dot 2 paper cups with gold glitter glue; let dry. Cut 2 slits, the width of ribbon, opposite each other below the rim of 1 cup. Cut 1 slit below the rim of the second cup. Place the* *center of the ribbon under the first cup. Bring ribbon ends up the sides of the cup and thread them through through the slits. Invert the second cup over the first; thread 1 ribbon end through the slit in the second cup, making a hinge on the container. Fill bottom cup with cheese. Bring together ribbon ends; tie them in a bow.*

Almond-Raisin Butter

This nutty, fruity spread tastes great on toast or pancakes. If you like, tailor it with dried fruit from your locality. Dried cranberries, blueberries, and tart red cherries all are excellent substitutes for the raisins.

Start to Finish: 15 minutes
Makes: 1 cup (about 24 servings)

- ½ cup butter, softened
- ½ cup chopped golden raisins
- 1½ teaspoons finely shredded orange peel
- 2 tablespoons orange juice
- 2 tablespoons sliced almonds, toasted (see note, page 131)

1. In a medium mixing bowl beat butter with an electric mixer on medium speed until light and fluffy. Add raisins, orange peel, orange juice, and almonds; stir until combined. Cover; refrigerate up to 1 week. Serve at room temperature.

Almond-Raisin Butter

Spicy Barbecue Rub

Spicy Barbecue Rub

Here's a welcome gift for barbecue enthusiasts on your list!

Prep: 5 minutes
Makes: about ⅓ cup seasoning

- 2 tablespoons packed brown sugar
- 1 tablespoon granulated sugar
- 1 tablespoon ground allspice
- 1 tablespoon ground ginger
- 1 teaspoon salt
- 1 teaspoon ground cumin
- 1 teaspoon cayenne pepper
- 1 teaspoon ground black pepper

1. In a small bowl stir together all the ingredients. Transfer to a small airtight container or self-sealing plastic bag. Store at room temperature up to 6 months. Attach Use Directions when offering as a gift.

Use Directions: *To use, sprinkle mixture evenly over meat, poultry, or fish before grilling. Rub in seasoning with your fingers.*

Note: *Spices lose flavor after 1 year. To ensure that your gift stays fresh for the 6 months indicated, use spices that have been recently purchased.*

Spinach, Arugula, and
Orange Pesto

running, gradually add the oil in a thin, steady stream, processing or blending until the mixture is combined and slightly chunky. Add cheese, orange peel, orange juice, cayenne pepper, and salt. Process or blend just until combined.

2. To store pesto, divide into ¼-cup portions and place in airtight containers. Store in refrigerator up to 1 week or in the freezer up to 3 months. Attach Use Directions if presenting as a gift. If using a jar with a cork lid, as shown, cover pesto with plastic wrap before adjusting lid.

*Note: *If using a blender, coarsely chop leaves for easier blending.*

Note: *To present as a gift, as shown at left, wash and dry a glass jar. Avoid touching surface areas to be painted. For large white dots, dip the handle end of a paintbrush into glass paints; dot paint on glass. Let the paint dry. For small center dots, dip a toothpick into paint; dot in the center of white. Let dry. Bake, cool, and care for the painted glassware as instructed by the paint manufacturer.*

For the beaded trim, cut a length of white plastic-coated crafting wire 8 inches longer than the circumference of the neck of the jar. Coil 1 end of the wire around a pencil or paintbrush handle; slip off. From the uncoiled wire end, thread beads on the wire, leaving 2 inches of wire unbeaded. Coil the end. Place the beaded wire around the neck of the jar. Twist the coiled ends together to secure.

Spinach, Arugula, and Orange Pesto

Choose whichever dark, leafy green is available at the market. Arugula, sorrel, and watercress all fare well in this perky version of pesto.

Prep: 20 minutes Makes: 1¼ cups

- ¼ **cup slivered almonds, toasted (see note, page 131)**
- 1½ **cups packed fresh spinach leaves***
- 1½ **cups packed fresh arugula, sorrel, or watercress leaves***
- ⅓ **cup olive oil**
- ⅓ **cup grated Parmesan or Romano cheese**
- ½ **teaspoon finely shredded orange peel**
- 3 **tablespoons orange juice**
- ¼ **teaspoon cayenne pepper**
- ¼ **teaspoon salt**

1. Place almonds in a food processor bowl or blender container. Cover and process or blend the almonds until finely chopped. Add the spinach and arugula; cover. With the machine

Use Directions: *Bring pesto to room temperature. Serve as a condiment for sandwiches or grilled meats, swirl it into soups and dips for added flavor, or toss with pasta for a main or side dish.*

Sweet Cherry Jam

Next summer preserve the sweetness of cherry season (late June and early July) in a jam everyone will cherish at Christmas.

Prep: 50 minutes Cook: 5 minutes
Makes: 6 half-pints (96 [1-tablespoon] servings)

- 3 **pounds fully ripe dark sweet cherries***
- 1 **1¾-ounce package regular powdered fruit pectin**

1   **teaspoon finely shredded lemon peel**
¼   **cup lemon juice**
5   **cups sugar**

1. Sort, wash, stem, pit, and chop the cherries. Measure 4 cups chopped cherries.

2. In a 6- or 8-quart Dutch oven combine cherries, pectin, lemon peel, and lemon juice. Bring to a full rolling boil (see first note, page 125) over high heat, stirring constantly. Stir in sugar. Return to a full rolling boil. Boil hard for 1 minute, stirring constantly. Remove from heat. Quickly skim off foam with a metal spoon.

3. Immediately ladle hot jam into hot, sterilized half-pint canning jars (see second note, page 125), leaving a ¼-inch headspace. Wipe jar rims and adjust lids. Process filled jars in a boiling-water canner for 5 minutes (start timing when water begins to boil). Remove jars from canner; cool on racks. Store in a cool, dry place. Refrigerate after opening.

*Note: *To easily remove pits from cherries, use a cherry pitter, available from cookware shops and catalogs. If you don't have a pitter, halve the cherries and pry out the pits with the tip of a knife.*

Note: *To present as a gift as shown below, use a pencil to trace around the inner jar lid onto the wrong side of wrapping paper. Cut a circle 1½ inches beyond the traced mark. Cut scallops along the edge of the paper circle. Evenly clip into the scalloped edges, clipping only to the first traced line (the inner jar lid). Place scalloped wrapping paper circle on the inner lid. Carefully screw on the top. Tie a narrow ribbon, with a card, around the jar lid. Present with a gold or silver serving spoon for an added touch.*

Sweet Cherry Jam

Sweet Potato-Banana Butter

2. Place drained sweet potatoes in a food processor bowl. Cover and process until smooth. Add the bananas; cover and process until smooth.

3. In a large saucepan stir together the sweet potato-banana mixture, brown sugar, honey, lemon juice, cinnamon, salt, ginger, and nutmeg. Bring to boiling; reduce heat. Cook, uncovered, over very low heat about 30 minutes or until very thick, stirring frequently.

4. Place the saucepan in a sink filled with ice water to cool the sweet potato mixture. Spoon cooled mixture into storage containers. Cover and store in the refrigerator up to 3 weeks.

Cranberry Conserve

When you've been invited to a turkey dinner feast, take along a jar of this conserve as a gift for the hosts. They'll love it first as a relish on the holiday table—and later served on leftover turkey sandwiches.

Prep: 45 minutes Cook: 20 minutes plus 5 minutes for processing
Makes: about 6 half-pints conserve

  4 cups fresh cranberries
1¼ cups water
  1 cup raisins
  1 tablespoon finely shredded orange peel
  2 oranges, peeled
2½ cups sugar
  1 cup chopped pecans, toasted (see note, page 131)

1. In a large saucepan combine cranberries, water, raisins, and orange peel. Slice oranges; cut each slice in quarters. Add orange pieces to cranberries in saucepan. Bring to boiling; reduce heat. Simmer, uncovered, about 10 minutes or until cranberries are soft, stirring occasionally.

2. Add sugar and pecans to cranberry mixture in saucepan. Stir until sugar dissolves. Bring mixture to a full rolling boil.* Reduce heat. Boil gently,

Sweet Potato-Banana Butter

Though sweet potatoes are available year-round, peak seasons are autumn and winter—a naturally good time to put this butter on your (or a friend's) holiday table.

Prep: 40 minutes Cook: 30 minutes
Makes: about 4 half-pints butter

  2 pounds sweet potatoes
     (about 4 medium)
  2 medium ripe bananas, cut up
1¼ cups packed brown sugar
⅔ cup honey
  2 tablespoons lemon juice
  1 teaspoon ground cinnamon
½ teaspoon salt
½ teaspoon ground ginger
¼ teaspoon ground nutmeg

1. Peel sweet potatoes; cut off woody portions and ends. Cut into quarters. Cook, covered, in enough boiling salted water to cover for 15 to 20 minutes or until tender; drain. Cool slightly.

uncovered, for 10 minutes, stirring occasionally. Remove from heat.

3. Immediately ladle conserve into hot, sterilized half-pint canning jars,** leaving a ½-inch headspace. Wipe jar rims; adjust lids. Process filled jars in a boiling-water canner for 5 minutes (start timing when water begins to boil). Remove from canner; cool on a wire rack. Store in a cool, dry place. Refrigerate after opening.

*Note: *A liquid is at a full rolling boil when the liquid is boiling so vigorously that the bubbles cannot be stirred down.*

**Note: *Use only standard canning jars to safely preserve conserves, jams, fillings, and preserves. To prepare canning jars, wash them in hot, soapy water and rinse thoroughly. Sterilize the jars by immersing them in boiling water for 10 minutes.*

Freezer Cranberry Conserve: *To freeze conserve, prepare as above, except ladle mixture into half-pint freezer containers, leaving a ½-inch headspace. Seal, label, and allow to cool slightly. Store up to 1 year in freezer or up to 3 weeks in refrigerator.*

Gingerberry Relish

Pineapple provides the tropical sweetness, and ginger creates a lively spark. Nut lovers will appreciate the extra texture and richness if you stir in ⅓ cup chopped walnuts right before serving.

Start to Finish: 25 minutes
Makes: 14 to 15 (¼-cup) servings

- 1 8¼-ounce can crushed pineapple (syrup pack)
- ⅔ cup sugar
- ½ cup water
- ¾ teaspoon ground ginger
- 1 12-ounce package (3 cups) cranberries

1. In a medium saucepan combine the undrained pineapple, sugar, water, and ginger. Cook and stir

over medium heat until sugar is dissolved. Add the cranberries.

2. Bring pineapple mixture to boiling; reduce heat. Cook and stir for 3 to 4 minutes more or until cranberries pop. Transfer to an airtight container. Cover and refrigerate up to 3 days.

Note: *To present Gingerberry Relish in a jar with beaded trim as shown below, cut a 16-inch length of wire. To secure the glass beads of various shapes and sizes, coil 1 end of the wire around an ice pick; remove the coiled wire from the ice pick. String on 3 inches of glass, seed, and gold beads. String 8 inches of seed beads in a pattern. Matching the first 3 inches of glass, seed, and gold beads, string the opposite wire end. Coil the wire end to match the first coiled end. Wrap the beaded wire around the neck of the glass jar; twist to secure.*

Gingerberry Relish

Honey-Pear Preserves

10 minutes (start timing when water begins to boil). Remove jars from canner; cool jars on wire racks. Store preserves in a cool, dry place. Refrigerate after opening.

Nectarine-Blueberry Pie Filling

Remember this recipe in the summer, when blueberries and nectarines are in season and schedules slow down a bit. If you take the time to make this luscious pie filling in the summer, it will be ready and waiting as the holiday season starts to get hectic.

Prep: 1 hour Cook: 30 minutes
Makes: 4 quarts (enough for 4 pies)

   5 **pounds fully ripe, firm nectarines**
      or peaches
      Ascorbic acid color keeper
   6 **cups fresh blueberries**
3½ **cups sugar**
1⅓ **cups quick-cooking tapioca**
   1 **teaspoon grated fresh ginger**
   ½ **teaspoon ground cinnamon**
   ⅛ **teaspoon ground nutmeg**
2¼ **cups water**
   ¾ **cup lemon juice**

1. Rinse nectarines; halve and remove pits. If using peaches, immerse in boiling water for 20 to 30 seconds or until skins begin to crack; remove and plunge into cold water. Slip off skins; halve and remove pits. Cut fruit into ½-inch slices. To prevent the fruit from darkening, treat it with ascorbic acid color keeper according to package directions. Measure 16 cups of nectarines or peaches. Rinse and drain blueberries. Set aside.

2. In an 8-quart Dutch oven heat about 6 cups water to boiling. Add half of the nectarines or peaches; return to boiling. Boil for 1 minute. Using a slotted spoon, transfer hot fruit to a large bowl; cover. Repeat with remaining nectarines or peaches. Discard liquid from Dutch oven.

3. In the same Dutch oven combine the sugar, tapioca, ginger, cinnamon, and nutmeg. Stir in the 2¼ cups water. Let stand for 5 minutes to allow tapioca to soften. Cook over medium-high

Honey-Pear Preserves

Many canning recipes are prepared during summer when fruits are at their freshest best. Thankfully pears are in season right around the holidays, so if you missed the summer canning season, you still have time to make home-preserved fruit for the holidays.

Prep: 30 minutes Cook: 30 minutes plus
10 minutes for processing Makes: 3 half-pints
(about 45 [1-tablespoon] servings)

   2 **to 3 pounds firm, ripe pears (such as**
      Bartlett or Bosc)
   1 **unpeeled lemon, quartered, seeded, and**
      very thinly sliced
1½ **cups sugar**
   ½ **cup honey**
   1 **teaspoon snipped fresh rosemary**

1. Core and peel pears. Finely chop enough pears to measure 4 cups. In a 4-quart Dutch oven, combine pears, lemon, sugar, and honey. Bring to boiling over medium heat, stirring until sugar is dissolved. Stir in rosemary. Boil gently, stirring frequently, for 20 to 25 minutes or until mixture is thickened and sheets off a metal spoon (2 drops of the mixture hang from the edge of spoon and run together in a sheetlike action).

2. Ladle hot preserves into hot, sterilized half-pint canning jars (see second note with Cranberry Conserve recipe, page 125), leaving a ½-inch headspace. Wipe jar rims; adjust lids. Process filled jars in a boiling-water canner for

heat, stirring constantly, until mixture thickens and begins to boil. Add lemon juice; boil for 1 minute, stirring constantly. Immediately add nectarines or peaches and blueberries, stirring gently to coat. Cook and stir for 3 minutes or until heated through.

4. Spoon hot fruit mixture into hot, sterilized quart-size canning jars (see second note with Cranberry Conserve recipe, page 125), leaving a 1½-inch headspace. Remove air bubbles, wipe jar rims, and adjust lids. Process filled jars in a boiling-water canner for 30 minutes (start timing when water begins to boil). Remove jars from canner; cool on wire racks. Attach Preparation Directions when offering gift.

Directions for Nectarine-Blueberry Pie: *Prepare pastry for two-crust pie. Spoon 1 quart Nectarine-Blueberry Pie Filling into a pastry-lined 9-inch pie plate. Cut slits in top crust; adjust top crust. Seal and flute edge. Cover edge of pie with foil. Bake in a 375°F oven for 25 minutes; remove foil. Bake for 25 to 30 minutes more or until pastry is golden and filling is bubbly. Makes 1 (9-inch) pie.*

Poinsettia-Shape Fruit Bread

Dried cranberries, golden raisins, and coarse sugar add extra sparkle to this unmistakable Christmas bread. The recipe makes three loaves—so you can share with friends and treat yourself as well. Pictured on page 117.

Prep: 50 minutes
Rise: 1½ hours plus 50 minutes
Bake: 20 minutes Stand: 10 minutes
Oven: 325°F Makes: 3 pinwheel loaves

  3¼ to 3¾ cups all-purpose flour
  2 packages active dry yeast
  ¾ cup milk
  ⅓ cup butter or margarine
  ⅓ cup granulated sugar
  1 teaspoon salt
  2 eggs
  ¾ cup golden raisins
  ¾ cup dried cranberries
  2 teaspoons finely shredded lemon peel

  1 slightly beaten egg white
  1 tablespoon water
     Coarse sugar

1. In a large mixing bowl combine 1½ cups of the flour and the yeast. In a medium saucepan heat and stir milk, butter, granulated sugar, and salt until warm (120°F to 130°F) and butter is almost melted. Add milk mixture to flour mixture along with the eggs. Beat with an electric mixer on low to medium speed for 30 seconds, scraping bowl. Beat on high speed for 3 minutes. Stir in raisins, dried cranberries, lemon peel, and as much of the remaining flour as you can.

2. Turn out dough onto a lightly floured surface. Knead in enough of the remaining flour to make a moderately soft dough that is smooth and elastic (3 to 5 minutes total). Shape into a ball. Place in a lightly greased bowl; turn once. Cover and let rise in a warm place until double (1½ to 2 hours).

3. Punch down dough. Turn out onto a lightly floured surface. Divide dough into thirds. Cover; let rest for 10 minutes. Grease 3 baking sheets.

4. Roll each portion of dough into an 8-inch square. Carefully transfer 1 square to a baking sheet, reshaping as necessary. Using a sharp knife, cut 4-inch slits from each corner to within ½ inch of the center of the square. Fold every other point to the center to form a pinwheel. Use water to moisten points of dough in center; press to seal. Repeat with remaining squares and baking sheets. Cover and let rise in a warm place until nearly double (about 50 minutes). Place 2 of the baking sheets, covered, in the refrigerator while the first loaf bakes.

5. Stir together egg white and water. Before baking, lightly brush egg white mixture on loaf. Sprinkle with coarse sugar. Bake, 1 loaf at a time, in a 325° oven for 20 to 25 minutes or until golden. Transfer pinwheel loaf to wire rack to cool. Repeat with remaining baking sheets from refrigerator. (Store egg white mixture, covered, in refrigerator when not in use.) Store loaves in airtight containers at room temperature up to 2 days or in the freezer up to 1 month.

New American Cuisine for the New Year

A GENERATION AGO CHEFS from the East and West Coasts and many major cities in between reinvented American cuisine, focusing on fresh, in-season produce enhanced with global ingredients. Chefs across the country continue to take American cuisine in exciting new directions, energizing it with their personal innovations. The fantastic party food featured here takes inspiration from the exciting fare served in today's dynamic bistros and other lively venues, providing you and your friends with new ways to ring in the New Year.

Rum-Glazed Short Ribs with Figs (recipe, page 134) and Gruyère-Garlic Mashed Potatoes (recipe, page 137)

Arugula Pesto Dip

The predominant herb in pesto was once fresh basil, but today's chefs have created innovative versions that include other herbs and greens. This dip follows their lead, calling on peppery arugula for flavor. While it makes a terrific dip, it's also good tossed with pasta for a sprightly side dish. Note: Thoroughly dry the leaves before pureeing the mixture in the food processor.

Prep: 25 minutes Makes: about 1 cup (eight 2-tablespoon servings)

1½ cups snipped fresh parsley
1 cup arugula
½ cup olive oil
⅓ cup pine nuts, toasted (see note, opposite)
¼ cup freshly grated Parmesan cheese
2 tablespoons lemon juice
¼ teaspoon salt
  Assorted vegetables such as endive, radishes, asparagus, yellow sweet pepper, and carrots

1. In a food processor bowl place parsley, arugula, oil, pine nuts, cheese, lemon juice, and salt. Cover and process until almost smooth. Transfer pesto to an airtight container. Refrigerate up to 3 days. If desired, bring to room temperature before serving. Serve with assorted vegetables.

Bacon 'n' Cheese Stuffed Dates

As chefs discover clever ways to tap into widely available world-class cheeses, some recipes are complex, but this one is easy. Sweet dates ooze with Cambozola cheese, which tastes like mild, creamy blue cheese.

Prep: 25 minutes Bake: 5 minutes
Oven: 350°F Makes: 24 appetizers

2 slices bacon, crisp-cooked, drained, and finely crumbled, or ¼ cup chopped prosciutto (2 ounces)
¼ cup thinly sliced green onions (2)
2 cloves garlic, minced
½ cup Cambozola cheese or crumbled blue cheese (2 ounces)
1 3-ounce package cream cheese, softened
2 teaspoons Dijon-style mustard
⅛ teaspoon ground black pepper
24 Medjool dates (16 ounces unpitted)

1. In a bowl stir together bacon, green onions, and garlic. Add Cambozola cheese, cream cheese, mustard, and pepper; stir to combine.

2. Cut a slit in each date; slightly spread open and remove pits. Fill with a rounded teaspoon of bacon mixture. Place dates, filling sides up, on a baking sheet. Bake in a 350° oven for 5 to 8 minutes or until heated through. Serve warm.

Classic Cocktails Once the domain of dark supper clubs and swanky dining rooms, cocktails are adding sparkle to the bright and airy atmosphere of today's casually stylish urban restaurants. Here's how to make three of the most popular standbys:

• **Martini:** In a cocktail shaker combine cracked ice, ¼ cup vodka or gin, and 1 tablespoon of dry vermouth (much less if you like your martini dry). Shake well to mix. Strain into a chilled cocktail glass. Garnish with a green olive or twist of lemon. Makes 1.

• **Daiquiri:** In a cocktail shaker combine cracked ice, 3 tablespoons light rum, 2 tablespoons lime juice, 1 teaspoon powdered sugar, and 1 teaspoon orange liqueur. Shake well to mix; strain into a chilled cocktail glass. Makes 1.

• **Margarita:** In a cocktail shaker combine cracked ice, 3 tablespoons tequila, 2 tablespoons triple sec, and 2 tablespoons lime juice. Shake well to mix. For a salt-rimmed glass, rub the edge of a chilled cocktail glass with a lime wedge; invert glass into a dish of coarse salt. Makes 1.

Onion-Fennel
Phyllo Cups

Amuse Bouche: At some high-end restaurants, guests enjoy an "amuse bouche" as they peruse the menu. The phrase means "amuse the mouth," which is what the bite-size appetizers do while guests await the delicacies to come. These yummy little tarts will definitely keep your guests amused for a while!

Onion-Fennel Phyllo Cups

Consider serving these savory bite-size tarts with a glass of sparkling pink champagne.

Prep: 25 minutes Cook: 16 minutes
Bake: 5 minutes Oven: 350°F
Makes: 30 appetizers

  2 tablespoons butter
  2 cups thinly sliced sweet onions
  1 cup thinly sliced fennel bulb
  ½ cup chopped walnuts, toasted*
  ¼ teaspoon salt
  ⅛ teaspoon ground black pepper
  2 2.1-ounce packages mini phyllo
     dough shells
  ½ cup finely shredded Gruyère cheese
     (2 ounces)

1. In a large skillet melt butter over medium-low heat. Add onions and fennel. Cook, covered, for 13 to 15 minutes or until onion mixture is tender

and begins to brown, stirring occasionally. Uncover; cook and stir over medium-high heat for 3 to 5 minutes or until golden brown. Spoon onion mixture into a small bowl. Snip onion mixture into small pieces. Stir in walnuts, salt, and pepper.

2. Place phyllo shells on a shallow baking pan. Spoon onion mixture evenly into shells. Sprinkle with cheese. Bake, uncovered, in a 350° oven for 5 to 8 minutes or until filling is heated through and cheese is melted. Serve warm.

Make-Ahead Tip: *Cover and chill filling up to 24 hours. Let filling stand for 15 minutes at room temperature; fill and bake phyllo shells as directed.*

***Note:** Toasting highlights the flavor of nuts and seeds. To toast, spread the nuts or seeds in a single layer in a shallow baking pan. Bake in a 350°F oven for 5 to 10 minutes or until light golden brown, watching carefully and stirring the food once or twice so it doesn't burn.*

Tossed Greens with Goat
Cheese Phyllo Packets

1. For vinaigrette, in a screw-top jar combine olive oil, vinegar, the 1 tablespoon chutney, shallot, salt, and pepper. Cover and shake well; set aside.

2. Unfold phyllo dough; cover with plastic wrap. Place 1 sheet of phyllo dough on a flat surface. Brush the phyllo dough with some of the melted butter, being sure to brush butter all the way to the edges. Repeat with remaining 2 sheets of phyllo dough and butter, stacking the phyllo sheets. Cut stack in half lengthwise and into 3 crosswise pieces to form 6 equal squares.

3. Slice cheese into 6 equal pieces. Place a slice in the center of each phyllo square; divide the 2 tablespoons of chutney on the cheese slices. Gather corners of phyllo dough up and around filling; gently pinch edges to seal. Gently brush any remaining butter on outsides of packets.

4. Arrange phyllo packets on a lightly greased baking sheet. Bake in a 350° oven for 15 to 20 minutes or until golden brown. Meanwhile, in a very large bowl combine greens, pear slices, and endive. Add vinaigrette; toss gently to coat. Divide salad among 6 plates. Top each with a warm phyllo packet.

Make-Ahead Tip: *Prepare as directed in steps 2 and 3. Chill, covered, up to 4 hours. To serve, bake packets as directed.*

Tossed Greens with Goat Cheese Phyllo Packets

New American chefs often put their own spin on classic dishes. Here, France's beloved goat cheese salad is transformed into a dish with soft cheese tucked inside phyllo packets.

Prep: 30 minutes Bake: 15 minutes Oven: 350°F
Makes: 6 servings

- 3 tablespoons extra-virgin olive oil
- 2 tablespoons balsamic vinegar
- 1 tablespoon mango chutney, snipped
- 1 teaspoon finely chopped shallot
- ¼ teaspoon salt
- ⅛ teaspoon freshly ground black pepper
- 3 sheets frozen phyllo dough (9×14-inch rectangles), thawed
- 2 tablespoons butter or margarine, melted
- 1 4-ounce log goat cheese with herbs
- 2 tablespoons mango chutney, snipped
- 1 5-ounce package mesclun greens or spring mix (about 5 cups)
- 2 pears, cored and thinly sliced
- 2 large heads Belgian endive, leaves separated

Asparagus Salad with Tarragon Vinaigrette

Today's chefs go well beyond the usual tossed salads, imbuing the greens with a world of great flavors. This salad follows that lead!

Start to Finish: 25 minutes Makes: 4 servings

- 1 pound fresh asparagus
- 2 tablespoons rice vinegar
- 2 tablespoons dry sherry or orange juice
- 1 teaspoon sugar
- 1 teaspoon snipped fresh tarragon or ¼ teaspoon dried tarragon, crushed
- ½ teaspoon Dijon-style mustard

⅛ teaspoon freshly ground black pepper
2 tablespoons olive oil
6 cups torn mixed salad greens
1 tablespoon sesame seeds, toasted (see note, page 131)

1. Snap off and discard woody bases from asparagus. If desired, scrape off scales. In a medium covered saucepan cook asparagus in a small amount of boiling water for 2 to 4 minutes or until crisp-tender. Transfer asparagus spears to a bowl filled with ice water; set aside.

2. For dressing, in a food processor bowl or blender container combine rice vinegar, sherry, sugar, tarragon, mustard, ⅛ teaspoon salt, and pepper. With processor or blender running, slowly add oil in a thin, steady stream. (This should take about 1 minute.) Continue processing or blending until well mixed.

3. To serve, drizzle about half of the dressing on the greens; toss to coat. Divide greens among 4 salad plates. Pat asparagus dry with paper towels; arrange on greens. Drizzle remaining dressing on asparagus; sprinkle with sesame seeds.

Baby Greens Salad with Oranges and Olives

Add the blood oranges just before serving. Overmixing causes their color to bleed.

Start to Finish: 15 minutes Makes: 8 servings

12 cups mesclun or other mild salad greens
3 tablespoons olive oil
2 tablespoons blood orange juice or regular orange juice
2 tablespoons balsamic vinegar
8 thin slices red onion, separated into rings
2 cups blood orange and/or regular orange sections (8 blood oranges or 6 regular oranges)
⅔ cup mixed country olives or regular kalamata olives

1. Place greens in a large salad bowl. For dressing, in a small bowl whisk together olive oil, orange juice, and vinegar. Pour dressing over greens; gently toss to mix. Divide mixture among 8 salad plates. Top with onion rings, orange sections, and olives. Sprinkle with ⅛ teaspoon *salt* and *pepper*.

Fresh Herb Vinaigrette

Great restaurants usually have their own versions of vinaigrette. Use this recipe, or the variations, to make your own house specialty.

Start to Finish: 10 minutes Makes: about ¾ cup

⅓ cup olive oil or salad oil
⅓ cup white or red wine vinegar, rice vinegar, or white vinegar
1 to 2 teaspoons sugar
1 tablespoon snipped fresh thyme, oregano, or basil, or ½ teaspoon dried thyme, oregano, or basil, crushed
¼ teaspoon dry mustard or 1 teaspoon Dijon-style mustard
1 clove garlic, minced

1. In a screw-top jar combine oil, vinegar, sugar, herb, mustard, garlic, and ⅛ teaspoon *ground black pepper*. Cover and shake well. Serve immediately or cover and store in refrigerator for up to 3 days if using fresh herbs. If using dried herbs, store covered in refrigerator up to 1 week. Shake before serving.

Balsamic Vinaigrette: *Prepare as above, except use regular or white balsamic vinegar instead of the listed vinegar options.*

Orange-Balsamic Vinaigrette: *Prepare Balsamic Vinaigrette as above, except reduce balsamic vinegar to 3 tablespoons. Add ½ teaspoon finely shredded orange peel and ¼ cup orange juice.*

Ginger Vinaigrette: *Prepare as above, except use rice vinegar, substitute 2 teaspoons honey for the sugar, and use 1 teaspoon grated fresh ginger instead of the herb. Add 2 teaspoons soy sauce.*

Apricot Vinaigrette: *Prepare as above, except use white wine vinegar and reduce amount to 2 tablespoons; add ⅓ cup apricot nectar.*

Bistro Cuts Many of today's chefs are tapping into the appeal of traditionally under-appreciated cuts of meats, such as short ribs, veal shanks, and pork shoulder. It's no wonder. After subjected to a slow, gentle braising, these cuts magically soften and become meltingly fork-tender, resulting in the kind of boldly flavored feel-good food cozy neighborhood venues serve. Happily, the same qualities that make them a boon to the bistro chef (they're cheap, low-maintenance, and never fail to satisfy) also make them a joy for home cooks. See just what we mean with Rum-Glazed Short Ribs with Figs. After a minimal amount of upfront prep, you can relax and let the dish braise for hours on its own while you get everything ready for a spirited, convivial evening.

Rum-Glazed Short Ribs with Figs

Here's a luscious way to serve a very bistro-esque cut of meat. For a great New Year's Eve dinner for six, serve with Tossed Greens with Goat Cheese Phyllo Packets, Gruyère-Garlic Mashed Potatoes, Garlicky Swiss Chard, and Tangy Lemon Tart (see recipes in this chapter). Pictured on page 129.

Prep: 15 minutes Bake: 3 hours
Oven: 325°F Makes: 6 servings

  4½ **pounds meaty beef short ribs (about 12)**
      Salt and ground black pepper
  2 **tablespoons cooking oil**
  1¼ **cups dried figs (about 6½ ounces)**
  1 **8-ounce can tomato sauce**
  ½ **cup dark rum**
  ¼ **cup honey**
  2 **tablespoons red wine vinegar**
  1 **tablespoon minced garlic (6 cloves)**
  1 **tablespoon dried herbes de Provence, crushed**
      Snipped fresh parsley

1. Season ribs with salt and pepper. In a 4-quart Dutch oven brown ribs, half at a time, in hot oil. Drain off fat. Return ribs to Dutch oven. Add figs to meat in Dutch oven.

2. For sauce, in a medium bowl stir together the tomato sauce, rum, honey, vinegar, garlic, and herbes de Provence. Pour sauce over ribs and figs, stirring to coat. Bake, covered, in a 325° oven for 3 hours or until meat is tender, stirring occasionally.

3. Use a slotted spoon to transfer ribs and figs to a serving dish; cover and keep warm. Spoon fat from sauce in Dutch oven. In a small saucepan bring sauce to boiling; boil gently, uncovered, for 5 to 10 minutes until desired consistency. Spoon over ribs. Garnish with snipped fresh parsley.

Spicy Pork Tenderloin with Lime Mayonnaise

When you host a New Year's Eve appetizer spread, guests appreciate a few substantial bites among lighter offerings. These zesty pork-filled buns satisfy hearty appetites, and the cool lime mayo is a lovely contrast to the spicy meat.

Prep: 30 minutes Roast: 25 minutes
Stand: 30 minutes Chill: Overnight
Oven: 425°F Makes: 30 to 32 appetizers

  1½ **teaspoons minced garlic (3 cloves)**
  1 **teaspoon paprika**
  ½ **teaspoon salt**
  ½ **teaspoon dried oregano, crushed**
  ½ **teaspoon ground cumin**
  ¼ **teaspoon cayenne pepper**
  ¼ **teaspoon ground black pepper**
  1 **12-ounce pork tenderloin**
  ½ **cup mayonnaise**
  ½ **teaspoon finely shredded lime peel**
  1 **tablespoon lime juice**
  30 **2-inch hors d'oeurve buns, split, or 30 to 32 ¼-inch slices baguette-style French bread**
      Lime wedges and cilantro (optional)

Spicy Pork Tenderloin with Lime Mayonnaise

Quality Meats Most chefs agree that it's equally important to start with the right ingredients as it is to know exactly how to prepare them in the kitchen. In their quest for the best-tasting meats and poultry, many chefs seek products from animals that were fed natural feeds, raised without growth-promoting hormones or antibiotics, and allowed to roam free rather than caged in confinements. Many chefs feel these practices are more humane and also result in richer, more marbled meats (in the case of beef and pork) and plumper, full-flavored chicken. If you'd like to try naturally raised meats in recipes such as Spicy Pork Tenderloin with Lime Mayonnaise, good sources include farmers' markets, natural food stores, and larger supermarkets. Also see Sources, page 156, for a mail order source.

1. In a small bowl combine garlic, paprika, salt, oregano, cumin, cayenne pepper, and black pepper. Rub garlic mixture all over the pork; wrap and refrigerate overnight.

2. Unwrap pork; place in a roasting pan. Roast pork in a 425° oven for 25 minutes or until a meat thermometer inserted in thickest part of tenderloin reaches 160°F. Let roasted pork stand for 30 minutes to cool.

3. Meanwhile, for lime mayonnaise, in a small bowl combine the mayonnaise, lime peel, and lime juice.

4. To serve, cut pork into very thin slices. Serve on hors d'oeuvre buns or open face on baguette-style French bread with lime mayonnaise. If desired, garnish with lime wedges and cilantro.

Make-Ahead Tip: *Roast pork and prepare mayonnaise as directed. Cover and chill separately up to 2 days. Let pork stand at room temperature for 30 minutes before serving.*

Baked Pasta with Mushrooms and Chard

Baked Pasta with Mushrooms and Chard

Not long ago, restaurants offered vegetarian diners few choices—with pasta and tomato sauce always at the top of the list! Now chefs take pride in making creative and varied meatless dishes. Filled with meaty mushrooms, vibrant chard, and plenty of rich, luscious cheese, this pasta pleases all guests—vegetarians and meat-eaters alike.

Prep: 45 minutes Bake: 30 minutes
Oven: 350°F Makes: 8 servings

   12 ounces dried ziti or penne pasta
       (about 3½ cups)
    1 15-ounce carton whole milk ricotta
       cheese
    1 cup half-and-half or light cream
    1 egg
    1 teaspoon sugar
   ½ teaspoon salt
   ¼ teaspoon freshly ground black pepper
   ⅛ teaspoon ground nutmeg

   ¼ cup snipped fresh thyme, parsley, basil,
       and/or rosemary
   ¼ cup cooking oil
    1 pound crimini mushrooms, sliced (about
       6 cups)
   12 ounces shiitake mushrooms, sliced
       (about 4½ cups)
   ¼ cup finely chopped shallots
    2 cloves garlic, minced
    4 cups chopped Swiss chard or spinach*
    2 cups shredded Gruyère cheese
       (8 ounces)
   ½ cup shredded Parmigiano-Reggiano
       cheese (½ ounce)

1. Cook pasta according to package directions; drain pasta.

2. Meanwhile, place the ricotta cheese in a food processor bowl; cover and process until smooth. Add half-and-half, egg, sugar, salt, pepper, and nutmeg; process until well blended. Stir in thyme. Stir cheese mixture into cooked pasta; set aside.

3. In a large skillet heat oil over medium-high heat. Add crimini mushrooms; cook and stir until

tender and liquid is reduced. Remove mushrooms from skillet. Add shiitake mushrooms, shallots, and garlic to skillet. Cook and stir until tender and liquid is reduced. Return crimini mushrooms to skillet; add Swiss chard. Cook and stir for 2 to 3 minutes or until chard is wilted. Drain mixture well in a colander or sieve. Stir into pasta mixture; stir in half of the Gruyère cheese. Transfer to a 3-quart rectangular baking dish.

4. Bake, covered, in 350° oven for 20 minutes. Sprinkle with remaining Gruyère cheese and the Parmigiano-Reggiano cheese. Bake, uncovered, for 10 to 15 minutes more or until heated through and the top begins to brown.

*Note: For best results, if using Swiss chard, use green rather than red; red colors the pasta a pinkish hue. If green chard is not available, use spinach.

Brussels Sprouts with Pancetta and Parmesan

It's amazing how chefs can take the least glamorous vegetables and really make them sing! Here Brussels sprouts take an amazing turn, thanks to an attractive way to cut them and irresistible flavorings.

Prep: 20 minutes Cook: 12 minutes
Makes: 6 servings

    2 ounces sliced pancetta (Italian bacon)
       or 3 slices bacon, diced
    1 clove garlic, minced
 1¼ pounds fresh Brussels sprouts, trimmed
       and cut into ¼-inch lengthwise slices
       (about 7 cups sliced)
  ¾ cup chicken broth
  ⅛ teaspoon salt
  ⅛ teaspoon freshly ground black pepper
  ¼ cup whipping cream
  ¼ cup finely shredded Parmesan cheese

1. In a 12-inch nonstick skillet cook pancetta over medium heat for 6 to 8 minutes until crisp (6 minutes for bacon). With a slotted spoon, transfer to a plate. Reserve 1 tablespoon of drippings in the skillet.

2. Add garlic to drippings in skillet; cook and stir for 30 seconds or until golden. Add Brussels sprouts, broth, salt, and pepper. Bring to boiling. Reduce heat to medium-low; cook, covered, for 5 to 7 minutes or until Brussels sprouts are just tender. Increase heat to medium-high.

3. Stir cream into Brussels sprouts mixture; cook, uncovered, for 1 minute more. Remove skillet from heat. Stir in pancetta and Parmesan cheese.

Gruyère-Garlic Mashed Potatoes

Bistros are known for homey, yearned-for foods—and mashed potatoes rank right up there when it comes to comfort. Of course, few chefs can resist imbuing the dish with their own touches. This recipe is truly creative with a little Gruyère in the mix. Pictured on page 129.

Prep: 20 minutes Cook: 20 minutes
Stand: 5 minutes Makes: 8 servings

 3½ pounds potatoes, peeled and cut into
       2-inch chunks (about 10 medium
       potatoes)
  ¼ cup butter
    2 cloves garlic, minced
  ½ cup whole milk, half-and-half, or
       light cream
  ¼ teaspoon salt
  ⅛ teaspoon ground black pepper
 1½ cups shredded Gruyère or Swiss cheese
       (6 ounces)

1. In a saucepan cook potatoes, covered, in a small amount of boiling lightly salted water for 20 to 25 minutes or until tender.

2. Meanwhile, in a small saucepan melt butter over medium heat. Add garlic to butter; cook for 2 minutes. Stir in milk, salt, and pepper. Cover; keep warm on very low heat. (Do not scorch.)

3. Drain potatoes; return to pan. Mash with a potato masher. Stir in warm garlic-milk mixture. Fold in cheese. Cover and let stand for 5 minutes to allow the cheese to melt.

Garlicky Swiss Chard

Chefs are bringing a whole new world of leafy greens to the table, including flavorful Swiss chard. Try this quick-cooking side dish with a dinner of long-braised meats, such as shanks, pork shoulder, or short ribs.

Prep: 10 minutes Cook: 15 minutes
Makes: 6 servings

- 3 **tablespoons olive oil**
- ¾ **cup thinly sliced onion**
- 3 **cloves garlic, minced**
- 3 **pounds green or red Swiss chard, rinsed, trimmed, and sliced 2 inches thick**
- ¼ **teaspoon salt**
- ¼ **teaspoon freshly ground black pepper**
  Salt and freshly ground black pepper (optional)

1. In a 6-quart Dutch oven heat oil over medium-high heat. Stir in onion; cover and cook for 5 minutes until tender, stirring occasionally. Add garlic; cook for 30 seconds. Increase heat to high; stir in half the Swiss chard, the ¼ teaspoon salt, and the ¼ teaspoon pepper. Cook, covered, for 2 minutes. Stir in remaining chard. Cook, covered, for 8 minutes more, stirring occasionally, until tender. If desired, season to taste with additional salt and pepper.

Potatoes Anna

Potatoes Anna is a classic French dish of stacked, fried potatoes. This version allows the bottom—which becomes the top when inverted—to brown to a lovely golden hue. For bistro-style presentation, use a large round cookie cutter to create 4 individual servings. If cut into wedges, you can serve up to 6. Serve with the Bistro Beef and Mushrooms, opposite.

Prep: 30 minutes Cook: 30 minutes
Stand: 5 minutes Makes: 4 to 6 servings

- 8 **medium red potatoes (about 3 pounds)**
- 4 **tablespoons butter**
- 1 **tablespoon cooking oil**
- ½ **teaspoon salt**
- ⅛ **teaspoon black pepper**

1. Scrub potatoes; remove eyes or sprouts. In a large saucepan cook potatoes, covered, in enough slightly salted water to cover about 25 minutes or until tender. Drain; cool until easy to handle. Peel potatoes and thinly slice.

2. In a heavy 12-inch skillet melt 3 tablespoons of the butter with the oil. Add half of the potatoes to the butter and oil in the skillet; dot with remaining 1 tablespoon of butter. Sprinkle with salt and pepper; top with remaining potatoes.

3. Cook, covered, over medium-low heat for 25 minutes or until heated through, occasionally pressing layers together. Increase heat to medium-high; cook for 3 to 5 minutes more or until bottom layer is browned. To serve, carefully invert pan onto a large cutting board or baking sheet; let stand for 5 minutes. Cut into 4 servings with a 4- to 5-inch round cookie cutter or cut into 4 to 6 wedges.

Bistro Beef and Mushrooms

Many American bistros look to France for inspiration, serving meals with classic French flair. This simple dish taps into Burgundy with Dijon mustard, red wine, and thyme. Serve it in the menu opposite. Or try it with mashed potatoes and buttered green beans any time of year. Why not follow this classic main course with a classic cheese course (see page 94)?

Start to Finish: 25 minutes
Makes: 4 servings

1 tablespoon Dijon-style mustard or coarse-grain brown mustard
4 4- to 5-ounce beef tenderloin steaks, cut to ¾-inch thickness
    Salt and ground black pepper
2 tablespoons olive oil or cooking oil
1 8-ounce package sliced shiitake,* crimini, or button mushrooms (about 3 cups)
⅓ cup dry red wine or beef broth
1 tablespoon white wine Worcestershire sauce
2 teaspoons snipped fresh thyme
    Salt and ground black pepper

1. Spread mustard evenly over both sides of steaks. Season steaks with salt and pepper. In a large skillet cook steaks over medium-high heat in 1 tablespoon of hot oil until desired doneness, turning once. Allow 7 to 9 minutes for medium rare (145°F) to medium (160°F). Transfer steaks to a serving platter; keep warm.

2. Add the remaining 1 tablespoon oil to drippings in skillet; add mushrooms. Cook and stir over medium-high heat for 4 minutes. Carefully stir in wine, Worcestershire sauce, and thyme. Cook and stir about 3 minutes or until mushroom mixture is reduced to desired consistency. Season to taste with salt and pepper; spoon over steaks.

*Note: Remove and discard stems from shiitake mushrooms, if using.

Bistro Beef and Mushrooms

What Is a Bistro? Many new American restaurants call themselves bistros, which is a very old term for such new venues. Some say the word originated with Russian soldiers who marched into Paris after Napoleon's defeat in 1815. Allegedly, when they arrived at the bars they shouted "bystro, bystro!"—which in Russian means "quickly, quickly." Whether they were demanding prompt service or—more likely—a quick-acting liquor called "bistouille" is not known.

Over the years the word eventually came to refer to a small informal restaurant where wine is served. Today, a traditional French bistro is a casual neighborhood restaurant in which locals convene over comfortingly familiar, homespun fare.

Some American bistros follow the traditional model of the French bistro, offering a menu filled with classic home-style French dishes. These might include such dishes as the Bistro Beef with Mushrooms, at left, Potatoes Anna, page 138, and a Tangy Lemon Tart, page 142. Other restaurateurs have taken the term bistro and run with it in different ways, putting their own spin on the concept. Such venues generally try to remain true to the warm, welcoming nature of the originals.

Lava Baby Cakes

Lava Baby Cakes

Recently, rich cakes with molten chocolate centers have emerged as one of the most popular restaurant desserts in years. The appeal is no surprise—few diners can resist a dessert that oozes with chocolate! The surprise? They're easy to make at home.

Prep: 15 minutes **Bake:** 13 minutes
Chill: 45 minutes **Oven:** 400°F
Makes: 6 servings

¾	**cup semisweet chocolate pieces (4½ ounces)**
2	**tablespoons whipping cream**
1	**cup semisweet chocolate pieces (6 ounces)**
¾	**cup butter**
3	**eggs**
3	**egg yolks**
⅓	**cup granulated sugar**
1½	**teaspoons vanilla**
⅓	**cup all-purpose flour**
3	**tablespoons unsweetened cocoa powder**
	Sifted powdered sugar (optional)
	Fresh raspberries (optional)

1. For filling, in a small heavy saucepan combine the ¾ cup chocolate pieces and whipping cream. Cook and stir over low heat until chocolate is melted. Remove from heat. Cool, stirring occasionally. Chill, covered, about 45 minutes or until firm.

2. Meanwhile, in a medium heavy saucepan cook and stir the remaining 1 cup chocolate pieces and butter over low heat until melted. Remove from heat; cool.

3. Form chilled filling into 6 equal-size balls; set aside. Lightly grease and flour six ¾-cup soufflé dishes or six 6-ounce custard cups. Place dishes or cups in a 15×10×1-inch baking pan; set aside.

4. In a medium mixing bowl beat eggs, egg yolks, granulated sugar, and vanilla with an electric

mixer on high speed for 5 minutes or until lemon color. Beat in cooled chocolate-butter mixture on medium speed. Sift flour and cocoa powder onto mixture; beat on low speed just until combined. Spoon ⅓ cup batter into dishes. Place 1 ball of filling into each dish. Spoon remaining batter into dishes.

5. Bake in a 400° oven about 13 minutes or until cakes feel firm at edges. Cool in dishes for 2 to 3 minutes. Using a knife, loosen cakes from sides of dishes. Invert onto dessert plates. If desired, dust with powdered sugar and garnish with raspberries. Serve immediately.

Make-Ahead Tip: *Prepare through step 4. Chill, covered, until ready to bake or up to 4 hours. Let stand at room temperature for 30 minutes before baking as directed.*

Lavender Crème Brûlée

Rarely content to let a classic stand, pastry chefs use the magic of herbs and fruit to put their personal stamp on crème brûlée. This version calls on lavender for the "wow—what is it?!" touch.

Prep: 20 minutes Bake: 30 minutes
Chill: 1 hour Stand: 20 minutes
Oven: 325°F Makes: 8 servings

2	to 3 teaspoons dried lavender flowers or 1 tablespoon snipped fresh basil
2	cups half-and-half or light cream
5	egg yolks, slightly beaten
⅓	cup sugar
1	teaspoon vanilla
⅛	teaspoon salt
⅓	cup sugar

1. In a heavy small saucepan heat dried flowers and half-and-half over medium-low heat just until bubbly. Remove from heat; strain through a fine mesh sieve; discard flowers; set aside flavored cream mixture.

2. Meanwhile, in a medium mixing bowl combine egg yolks, the ⅓ cup sugar, vanilla, and salt. Beat with a wire whisk or rotary beater just until combined. Slowly whisk the hot flavored cream mixture into the egg mixture.

3. Place eight 4-ounce ramekins or six 6-ounce custard cups in a 13×9×2-inch baking pan; place baking pan on the oven rack. Evenly pour custard mixture into the dishes. Pour boiling water into the baking pan around the dishes to reach halfway up the sides of the dishes (about 1 inch deep).

4. Bake the custards in a 325° oven for 30 to 35 minutes or until a knife inserted near center of each custard comes out clean. Remove custards from the water bath; cool on a wire rack. Cover and chill at least 1 hour or up to 8 hours.

5. Before serving, remove custards from the refrigerator; let stand at room temperature for 20 minutes. Meanwhile, place the remaining ⅓ cup sugar in a heavy medium or large skillet. Heat skillet over medium-high heat until sugar begins to melt; do not stir. Once the sugar starts to melt, reduce heat to low; cook about 5 minutes more or until all the sugar is melted and golden, stirring as needed with a wooden spoon.

6. Quickly drizzle the caramelized sugar over the custards. If sugar begins to harden in the skillet, return to heat, stirring until melted. Serve immediately.

Lavender Crème Brûlée

Tangy Lemon Tart

For a luscious, lively way to end a dinner party, serve this bistro-style lemon tart. It's especially refreshing after a hearty meal.

Prep: 45 minutes Bake: 15 minutes
Chill: 4 hours Oven: 450°F
Makes: 10 to 12 servings

  1½ **cups all-purpose flour**
  2 **teaspoons sugar**
  ½ **teaspoon salt**
  ⅓ **cup shortening**
  ¼ **cup cold butter**
  3 **to 4 tablespoons ice water**
  1¼ **cups sugar**
  ¼ **cup cornstarch**
  ⅛ **teaspoon salt**
  2 **teaspoons finely shredded lemon peel**
  ¾ **cup lemon juice**
  ⅓ **cup butter, cubed**
  ⅓ **cup water**
  5 **egg yolks**
     Candied Lemon Slices
  3 **tablespoons orange marmalade, melted**

1. For the crust, in a bowl combine flour, the 2 teaspoons sugar, and the ½ teaspoon salt. Use a pastry blender to cut shortening and the ¼ cup butter into flour mixture until mixture resembles coarse crumbs. Sprinkle 1 tablespoon of the water over part of the mixture; gently toss with a fork. Push moistened dough to side of bowl. Repeat, using 1 tablespoon water at a time, until all the dough is moistened. Shape dough into a ball.

2. Place dough between 2 sheets of waxed paper; roll from center to edge to form a 12-inch circle. Remove top sheet of waxed paper; invert pastry into a 10-inch tart pan with removable bottom. Peel off waxed paper. Ease pastry into pan; trim.

3. Line pastry with a double thickness of foil. Bake in a 450° oven for 8 to 10 minutes. Remove foil. Bake for 5 to 6 minutes more or until crust is golden brown. Set aside.

4. For lemon curd, in a medium saucepan stir together the 1¼ cups sugar, cornstarch, and the ⅛ teaspoon salt. Stir in lemon peel, lemon juice, the ⅓ cup butter, and the ⅓ cup water. Cook and stir until thickened and bubbly. Place the egg yolks in a bowl. Gradually stir about 1 cup of the hot lemon mixture into egg yolks. Pour all of the egg yolk mixture into the saucepan. Cook over medium heat until the lemon and egg yolk mixture just begins to bubble. Reduce heat; cook and stir for 2 minutes more.

5. Pour hot lemon curd into crust. Cool on a wire rack. Top cooled tart with Candied Lemon Slices, forming a ring of overlapping slices in the center. Lightly brush top of tart with melted orange marmalade. Cover; chill in the refrigerator at least 4 hours or up to 24 hours.

Candied Lemon Slices: *In a small saucepan combine ¼ cup sugar and ¼ cup water; bring to boiling. Add 8 very thin lemon slices. Simmer gently, uncovered, for 12 to 15 minutes or until softened and white portion of lemon slices become almost opaque. With a fork, transfer slices to waxed paper to cool. Discard any remaining syrup.*

Ginger-Scented Fig Tart

Hint: The dough may seem crumbly at first but will come together as you knead it.

Prep: 45 minutes Bake: 25 minutes
Cool: 15 minutes plus 2 hours
Oven: 375°F/350°F Makes: 8 servings

  1½ **cups all-purpose flour**
  ¼ **cup sugar**
  ¼ **teaspoon salt**
  ¾ **cup butter, cut into ½-inch slices**
  1 **egg yolk**
  2 **tablespoons cold water**
  1 **9-ounce package dried figs, coarsely snipped (2 cups)**
  ¾ **cup sugar**
  ½ **cup water**
  3 **tablespoons finely chopped crystallized ginger**
  2 **teaspoons finely shredded lemon peel**
     Whipped cream (optional)

Finely chopped crystallized ginger (optional)

1. For crust, in a large bowl stir together flour, the ¼ cup sugar, and salt. Using a pastry blender, cut butter into flour mixture until pieces are the size of peas. In a small bowl stir together egg yolk and 2 tablespoons water. Gradually stir egg yolk mixture into flour mixture. Using hands, gently knead the dough just until a ball forms (dough is crumbly at first and comes together as you knead.

2. Press dough evenly onto the bottom and up the sides of an ungreased 9-inch tart pan with a removable bottom. Prick bottom of crust with fork. Place pan with crust on a foil-lined baking sheet. Bake crust in a 375° for 18 to 20 minutes or just until golden. Remove from oven. Reduce oven temperature to 350°.

3. Meanwhile, for filling, place fig pieces in a medium bowl. Add enough boiling water to cover. Cover and let stand for 15 minutes; drain well and set aside. In a small saucepan combine the ¾ cup sugar, ½ cup water, the 3 tablespoons ginger, and lemon peel. Bring to boiling over medium-high heat, stirring to dissolve sugar; reduce heat. Simmer, uncovered, for 15 minutes or until syrup is thickened and reduced to about ⅔ cup, stirring occasionally. Cool syrup slightly (about 15 minutes); stir in drained figs. Spoon mixture into baked crust.

4. Bake tart on the foil-lined baking sheet for 25 to 30 minutes or until syrup is bubbly across the surface of the tart. Cool completely on a wire rack. If desired, serve with whipped cream and sprinkle with additional crystallized ginger.

Figs Ever been to California during fresh fig season? If so, you've likely seen them prominently featured on the menu. California grows more figs than any other state, so it follows that California chefs have developed dazzling ways to star the luscious, sweet fruit in both sweet and savory dishes. Because fresh figs are available only from June through October, the irresistible Ginger-Scented Fig Tart and the Rum-Glazed Short Ribs with Figs, page 134, call on dried figs, which are available year-round.

Ginger-Scented Fig Tart

Gingerbread Nativity Scene

FOR GENERATIONS crafting a gingerbread house for a tabletop display has been a way to bring a festive touch to the season. This project combines that tradition with another—the re-creation of the nativity scene, which for centuries has been a meaningful way to remember the humble and awe-inspiring origins of the first Christmas. In keeping with the simple nature of Christ's birth, this is an easy project to make. Call on one simple grid for the pattern, and search local shops for cookie cutters depicting the farm animals and nativity shapes for your own one-of-a-kind vision of the first Christmas.

Gingerbread Manger and Cookie Cutouts

Gingerbread Manger
- ¼ **cup shortening**
- ¼ **cup sugar**
- ½ **teaspoon baking powder**
- ½ **teaspoon ground ginger**
- ¼ **teaspoon baking soda**
- ¼ **teaspoon ground cinnamon**
- ¼ **teaspoon ground cloves**
- ¼ **cup molasses**
- ½ **egg or 2 tablespoons refrigerated or frozen egg product, thawed**
- 1½ **teaspoons vinegar**
- 1¼ **cups all-purpose flour**

Nativity and Farm Animal Shapes:
- ½ **recipe Sugar Cookie Cutouts (recipe, page 148)**

1. In a medium mixing bowl beat shortening with an electric mixer on medium to high speed for 30 seconds. Add sugar, baking powder, ginger, baking soda, cinnamon, and cloves. Beat until combined, scraping sides of bowl occasionally. Beat in molasses, egg, and vinegar. Beat in as much of the flour as you can with mixer. Using a wooden spoon, stir in any remaining flour. Cover and chill about 3 hours or until dough is easy to handle.

2. Enlarge the patterns on page 148 as directed. If desired, cover both sides of pattern pieces with clear adhesive plastic to protect them. Lightly grease the back of a 15×10×1-inch baking pan. If desired, place the pan on a damp towel to prevent it from sliding around.

3. Roll some of the gingerbread cookie dough to ¼-inch thickness on the greased pan. Place pattern pieces 1 inch apart on dough. Cut around patterns with a sharp knife. Remove excess dough, leaving dough cutouts on pan.

4. Bake in a 375° oven for 10 to 12 minutes or until edges are lightly browned and centers are just firm. Leaving warm, baked gingerbread on the pan, replace pattern pieces and trim edges exactly. Return trimmed gingerbread to oven and bake for 3 minutes more or until very firm. Cool

3 minutes on pan. Loosen bottoms of gingerbread pieces with a spatula. Cool completely on pan; transfer to wire racks. Repeat with the remaining dough and patterns.

5. Follow directions in step 1 of Sugar Cookie Cutouts. Cover and chill, if necessary, until dough is easy to handle. On a lightly floured surface, roll to ⅛-inch thickness. Using cookie cutters in nativity and farm animal shapes, cut out dough. Place on an ungreased cookie sheet.

6. Bake in a 375° oven for 7 to 8 minutes or until edges are firm and bottoms are very lightly browned. Transfer cookies to a wire rack; cool.

Nativity Scene Decorating and Assembling

Decorations
- 1 **recipe Royal Icing (recipe, page 149)**
  Paste food coloring
  Colored sugars and/or sanding sugar
  Flaked coconut
  Liquid yellow food coloring
  Large pretzel sticks or crisp breadsticks
  Graham crackers

To decorate and assemble nativity scene:
Assemble and display the nativity scene on waxed paper on a large tray or wooden cutting board. Pipe Royal Icing from a decorating bag (no couplers or tips are needed) or spread icing to fasten pieces together. Experiment to find the right amount of icing to use. If you apply too little icing, the pieces won't stay together, yet too much icing takes too long to dry. Let each set of pieces stand about 1 hour or until the icing is dry before continuing.

1. Prepare Royal Icing. Divide it into about 7 portions. Tint as desired with paste food coloring, leaving 1 portion white. (The scene shown uses blue, pink, green, yellow, ivory, and brown.) Place a small amount of each color in a decorating bag; set aside. Thin the remaining portions of icing until of spreading consistency.

2. Use thinned icing to frost the cutouts. If desired, use a small artist's paintbrush to paint multiple colors of icing. Let the icing dry thoroughly before adding detail trims. Snip the tips of the decorating bags filled with tinted icing. Pipe outlines and details onto cookies. While piped icing is still wet, immediately sprinkle colored sugar or sanding sugar onto icing. Shake off excess. Set cookies aside to dry.

3. For bales of straw, place coconut in a large plastic bag. Place several drops of yellow liquid food coloring in a ¼ teaspoon measure. Fill measure with water. Add to coconut in bag. Close bag and shake vigorously. With hands, gather yellow coconut into balls and mold into bale shapes. Cover until needed.

4. Attach two manger side walls to the back wall with icing; use glass measuring cups or heavy coffee mugs to hold pieces upright and steady until icing dries.

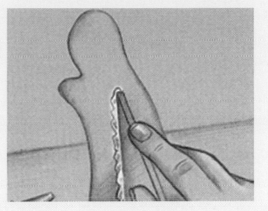

5. For the center vertical roof post, cut a large pretzel stick to 6½ inches. Prop the center post up using cups or mugs. For the roof beam, attach a whole large pretzel stick, resting one end on the post top and one on top of the back wall; let dry a few minutes. Beginning at front and alternating sides, lay large pretzel stick "logs" that stretch from the roof beam to the side walls (see illustration, top). The roof logs will have large spaces between them. If desired, attach some cut pretzels to front edges of gingerbread walls to finish them. Attach a decorated star cookie with icing at top of roof.

6. When icing on cookie cutouts is dry, carefully place cookies, decorated side down, on a work surface. Cut graham crackers into small triangles. Attach them at right angles near the bottoms of cookies for stands to keep the characters upright (see illustration, bottom). Let dry 1 or 2 hours before standing cookies up.

7. Arrange bales of straw, animals, and other cookie cutouts inside and around the manger. Add additional pretzels to look like wood pieces, if desired. You can also use candies and additional piped icing to decorate pretzel logs for manger interior, if desired.

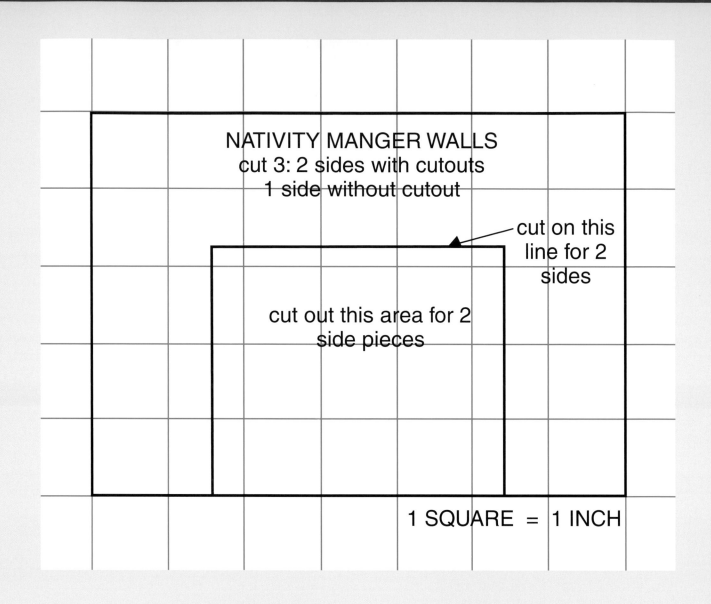

NATIVITY MANGER WALLS
cut 3: 2 sides with cutouts
1 side without cutout

cut on this line for 2 sides

cut out this area for 2 side pieces

1 SQUARE = 1 INCH

Sugar Cookie Cutouts

To make the Nativity and Farm Animal Shapes for the Gingerbread Nativity Scene, you only need half the dough. Use the other half of the dough to make classic Christmas cookie cutouts your family will love.

Prep: 35 minutes   Chill: 1¼ hours
Bake: 7 minutes per batch   Cool: 1 minute
Oven: 375°F

⅓ **cup butter, softened**
⅓ **cup shortening**
¾ **cup sugar**

1 **teaspoon baking powder**
   Dash salt
1 **egg**
1 **teaspoon vanilla**
2 **cups all-purpose flour**

1. In a medium mixing bowl beat butter and shortening with an electric mixer on medium to high speed for 30 seconds. Add sugar, baking powder, and salt. Beat until combined, scraping sides of bowl occasionally. Beat in egg and vanilla until combined. Beat in as much of the flour as you can with the mixer. Using a wooden spoon, stir in any remaining flour.

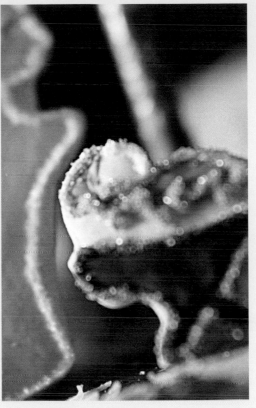

2. Cover and chill dough about 1 hour or until dough is easy to handle.

3. On a lightly floured surface, roll a portion of the dough at a time to ⅛-inch thickness. Using a 2½-inch cookie cutter, cut dough into desired shapes. (For 5¼-inch cookies, roll dough to ¼-inch thickness.) Place cutouts on an ungreased cookie sheet. Refrigerate cutouts for 15 minutes.

4. Bake in a 375° oven for 7 to 8 minutes for smaller cookies or about 10 minutes for larger cookies or until edges are firm and bottoms are very lightly browned. Cool on cookie sheet for 1 minute. Transfer cookies to a wire rack; cool. Makes about 48 (2½-inch) cookies or about 16 (5¼-inch) cookies.

Royal Icing

3 tablespoons meringue powder
⅓ cup warm water
1 16-ounce package powdered sugar, sifted (about 4¾ cups)
1 teaspoon vanilla
½ teaspoon cream of tartar
Paste food coloring

1. In a large mixing bowl combine meringue powder, water, powdered sugar, vanilla, and cream of tartar. Beat with an electric mixer on low speed until combined; then beat on high speed for 7 to 10 minutes or until very stiff. When not using icing, keep bowl covered with plastic wrap to prevent icing from drying out; keep icing refrigerated until needed. Makes 3 cups.

Nature's
Beauty
on Your
Table

TURN TO NATURE for an abundance of seasonal finery, and turn to this chapter for beautiful ways to star it on your holiday table. A lick of gold paint transforms Oregon pears into jewel-like treasures, while unadorned tropical fruits really brighten the centerpiece. From clever ways with cranberries to winsome ways with apples, squash, and citrus, you'll find a harvest of ideas to showcase the bounty of our fields, farms, and orchards.

LUSCIOUS FRUIT TREE—Decorate your buffet table with this fresh fruit centerpiece. Create the arrangement by topping a clear-glass-foot cake plate with a pineapple and surrounding it with the most colorful fruits you can find. Here red apples, red grapes, red and green Anjou pears, and kumquats fill the plate. Sprigs of pepper berries (available from florists) add a festive touch. For a taller, more pronounced tree, stack a smaller cake plate on top of a larger one and top off the glass tree with a footed candy dish. Fill in all three layers with fruit.

Luscious Fruit Tree

CHAIR STOCKING—The dining room chairs will look as attractive as your decked-out holiday table when you tie a traditional Christmas stocking onto each chair back and stuff it with irresistible treats. Stich a stocking out of a red and white vintage towel, then fill it with wrapped candies and nuts or a few of your favorite Christmas flowers. If you stitch a guest's name or initials to the stocking front, it will also serve as a place card and a party favor.

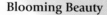

Blooming Beauty

Chair Stocking

BLOOMING BEAUTY—In addition to starring in delicious relishes, salads, and desserts throughout the season, cranberries from Northern bogs can add color when decorating the table and home. Here, the ruby-red gems make a beautiful ground cover from which fresh, bright stands of pretty paperwhite Narcissus bloom. To make this project, be sure to plan ahead. Four to six weeks before you want blooms, plant bulbs on gravel in a shallow bowl. Water the bulbs as needed, keeping the water level just below the bottom of the bulbs. When you're ready to display the flowers, cover the gravel with a few handfuls of fresh cranberries. Another idea: Use smaller vessels and plant just one or two bulbs in each, then offer the little planted pots as party favors. You can also add tags to each pot so the favor can double as a place card on your table.

GILDED PEARS—Pears brighten side tables or the mantel top when gilded with gold paint. Use spray paint or metal leaf from a crafts supply store to gild fresh or artificial pears. For a more subdued gold, brush each gilded pear with brown acrylic paint, quickly wiping off most of the brown paint so it tones down the gold color without covering it. Note: Fresh pears aren't suitable for eating after they've been gilded. Display the pears in a wooden, glass, or ceramic bowl surrounded by a combination of fresh evergreen sprigs, pinecones, and gilded greenery.

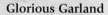

Glorious Garland

GLORIOUS GARLAND—Fresh Florida fruits adorn this luscious tabletop garland. To make a similar garland for your table, cut a piece of fresh evergreen garland to a length approximately 2 feet shorter than your table, then spread the garland onto the table into a gentle S-shape curve. Tuck a few ivy tendrils into the greens. Adorn the shapely greenery with a centerpiece of honeydew melon, cut open as shown, then add bunches of grapes, pomelo (a large citrus fruit), star fruit, quince, pears, and apples. Garnish the fruit garland with a few stems of your favorite flowers. Pink and white alstroemeria provides the crowning touch here. For a longer-lasting garland, tuck small pots of ivy into the evergreens and don't cut the fruit. Use dried or silk flowers in place of the fresh ones. Note: Never leave burning candles unattended.

Apple Art

APPLE ART—Fresh-from-the-orchard apples make a colorful display when the apples are decorated with simple painted patterns. Use a small brush and acrylic paint thinned with water to achieve a creamy consistency and paint the apples with whatever designs inspire you. (Here, the apples feature dots and scallops often seen on Scandinavian furniture.) Note that apples aren't suitable for eating after they've been painted.

Fine Wine

FINE WINE—Wine becomes another surprise package to open when you wrap it in ribbons and label it with a circular tag from an office supply store. To cover a wine bottle as shown, lay 16 feet of 3-inch-wide ribbon on a flat surface. Stand wine bottle upright on top and in the middle of the ribbon. Bring several inches of ribbon up flat along both sides of the bottle and secure to neck of bottle with a bead of hot glue. Keeping ribbon flat to the bottle, wrap one length of ribbon around the bottle, starting at the top, moving down the bottle with a few loose wraps, then back up again with tighter overlapping wraps and finishing near top of bottle. Repeat with ribbon from other side, making sure to completely cover the bottle. Tie both ends of ribbon in a knot at top of bottle. Use a 30-inch strip of ribbon to tie a bow at top of bottle.

Make matching wine tags for the bottle and glasses using prepunched circular silver-cased tags from office supply stores. Use a fine-point permanent marker to write a name, wine variety, or festive message onto each tag. On an 8-inch piece of thin wire, string a variety of color-coordinating beads. For the wineglass placeholders, string the tag at the end of the beaded wire. With tag at top, twist beaded wire around the stem of a glass, starting at the bottom and moving up. For the wine bottle tag, secure the tag in the middle of the beaded wire, place around the neck of a wine bottle, and secure at back of bottle by twisting ends of wire.

SOURCES

For this cookbook we've chosen many regionally distinct foods, most of which are widely available at well-stocked supermarkets. However, if you have difficulty finding a particular product or ingredient, the sources on this page may help.

CHEESE

Look for artisanal cheeses in well-stocked supermarkets and specialty cheese shops. Or contact producers for information on the availability of their cheeses in your area or to order from them directly.

Cabot Cheddar: 800/639-3198; www.cabotcheese.com
Capriole Goat Cheese: 812/923-9408;
    www.capriolegoatcheese.com
Crowley Cheese: 800/683-2606;
    www.crowleycheese-vermont.com
Laura Chenel's Chèvre: 707/996-4477
Major Farm Vermont Shepherd Sheep's Milk Cheese:
    802/ 387-4473; www.vermontshepherd.com
Point Reyes Original Blue Cheese:
    www.pointreyescheese.com; 800/591-6878
Shelburne Farms Cheddar: 802/985-8686;
    www.shelburnefarms.org
Vella Dry Jack Cheese: 800/848-0505

NATURALLY RAISED MEATS

Farmer's markets and health food stores are good local sources for naturally raised meats. Also try:
Niman Ranch: www.nimanranch.com

SMOKED SALMON

Find smoked salmon at well-stocked supermarkets and seafood markets. Mail order sources include:
Harry & David: 877/322-1200; www.harryanddavid.com

WINES

For further information on wines featured in "American Wines for Your Holiday Table," peruse these websites:

Barefoot Cellars: www.barefootwine.com
Beringer Vineyards (for Stone Cellars wines):
    www.beringer.com
Blackstone Winery: www.blackstonewinery.com
Bonny Doon Vineyard: www.bonnydoonvineyard.com
Buena Vista Winery: www.buenavistawinery.com
Cakebread Cellars: www.cakebread.com
Canyon Road Winery: www.canyonroadwinery.com
Chandon: www.chandon.com
Chateau St. Michelle Winery: www.chateaustemichelle.com
Chateau Souverain: www.chateausouverain.com
Columbia Winery: www.columbiawinery.com
Dry Creek Vineyard: www.drycreekvineyard.com
Forest Glen Winery: www.forestglenwinery.com
Gallo of Sonoma Barrelli Creek Vineyard
    www.gallosonoma.com
Geyser Peak Winery: www.geyserpeakwinery.com
Hawk Crest California Wines: www.cask23.com
Heron Wines: www.heronwines.com
Inglenook: www.inglenook.com
Kendall-Jackson Wine Estates: www.kj.com
Korbel: www.korbel.com
Meridian Vineyards: www.meridianvineyards.com
Mumm Cuvée Napa: www.mummcuveenapa.com
Niebaum-Coppola Estate Vineyards and Winery (for Sofia
    Blanc de Blancs): www.niebaum-coppola.com
Ravenswood Winery: www.ravenswood-wine.com
Robert Hall Winery: www.roberthallwinery.com
Robert Mondavi: www.robertmondavi.com
Roederer Estate: www.roedererestate.net
Rombauer Vineyards: www.rombauer.com
St. Supéry Vineyards and Winery: www.StSupery.com
Sanford Winery and Vineyards: www.sanfordwinery.com
Snoqualmie Vineyards: www.snoqualmie.com
Toasted Head Wines: www.toastedhead.com
Trinchero Family Estates: www.tfewines.com

INDEX

Note: *Pages in italics refer to photographs when pictured on a different page from recipes.*

A-B

J-O

Jellies and Jams
Cranberry Conserve, 124
Freezer Cranberry Conserve, 125
Honey-Pear Preserves, 126
Sweet Cherry Jam, 122
Key Lime Danish Pastries, 62
King Ranch Casserole, 56
Lady Baltimore Cookies, 100
Lamb, Stuffed Leg of, 14
Lava Baby Cakes 140
Lavender Crème Brûlée, 141
Lemons
Lemon Butter, 61
Lemon Glaze, 61
Lemon-Thyme Scones, 61
Tangy Lemon Tart, 142
Lime Zingers, 102
Lobster Bisque, 8
Luscious Orange Sponge Cake, 76
Macadamia Nuts
Chocolate-Dipped Nuts, 118
Honey-Macadamia Nut Fudge, 118
Orange and Macadamia Nut Cookies, 109
Mandarin Apricot Chicken Wings, 31
Maple
Maple-Apple Slump, 70
Maple Butter Cookies, 100
Mapled Brie and Apples, 32, 33
Maple-Glazed Turkey with Orange-Parsley Stuffing, 12
Maple Streusel Cake, 73
Margarita, 130
Martini, 130
Meat *(see Beef, Ham, Lamb, Pork, Sausage)*
Meringue Powder Icing, 106
Mexicitos, 42
Mushrooms
Asiago Cheese Dip, 87
Baked Pasta with Mushrooms and Chard, 136
Bistro Beef and Mushrooms, 139
Cheesy Wild Rice Casserole, 19
Fresh Mushroom Soup, 10
Mushrooms Filled with Ham and Blue Cheese, 40
Polenta Cheese Circles, 90
Potato-Parsnip Puree, 21
Sheep's Milk Cheese Antipasto Bowl, 91
Slow-Cooker Creamy Wild Rice Pilaf, 24
Nachos, Crowley Cheese, 88
Nectarine-Blueberry Pie Filling, 126
Nutty Orange Loaf, 64
Nutty Raisin Cream Pie, 79
Olives
Baby Greens Salad with Oranges and Olives, 133
Polenta Cheese Circles, 90
Sheep's Milk Cheese Antipasto Bowl, 91
Southwestern Quiche, 54
Ol' South Pralines, 119
Onion-Fennel Phyllo Cups, 131
Orange and Macadamia Nut Cookies, 109
Orange-Balsamic Vinaigrette, 133
Orange Butter, 64
Orange-Coconut Bars, 103
Orange Frosting, 109
Orange Glaze, 63

Oranges
Baby Greens Salad with Oranges and Olives, 133
Cranberry Conserve, 124
Nutty Orange Loaf, 64
Southern Ambrosia, 16
Winter Fruit Cup, 53
Orange Sauce, 49
Orange Whipped Cream, 76
Orchard Pear Tart, 82, 69

P-R

Pancakes, Blueberry-Cornmeal, 49
Pan Gravy, 24
Pastries
Baked Pastry Shell, 51
Key Lime Danish Pastries, 62
Pastry for Double-Crust Pie, 71, 75, 81
Pastry for Single-Crust Pie, 78
Pears
Cranberry-Pear Pie, 80
Honey-Pear Preserves, 126
Orchard Pear Tart, 82, 69
Poires Belle Hélène, 82, 83
Tossed Greens with Goat Cheese Phyllo Packets, 132
Pecans
Best-Ever Bourbon Brownies, 74
Chocolate-Dipped Nuts, 118
Coconut-Pecan Sticky Rolls, 65
Cranberry Conserve, 124
Creamy Cranberry Salad, 17
Dried Cherry Deluxe Cookies, 106
Grapefruit-Cranberry Drops, 102
Hickory Nut Salad with Apples, 9
Honey-Macadamia Nut Fudge, 118
Lady Baltimore Cookies, 100
Maple-Apple Slump, 70
Maple Streusel Cake, 73
Nutty Orange Loaf, 64
Nutty Raisin Cream Pie, 79
Ol' South Pralines, 119
Orange-Coconut Bars, 103
Pecan-Crusted Artichoke Dip, 38
Praline-Yam Casserole, 23
Stuffed Date Drops, 108
Sugar-Glazed Pecans, 81
Texas Red Grapefruit Salad, 16
Whiskey Laced Party Pecans, 39
Pesto, Spinach, Arugula, and Orange, 122
Pies and Tarts
Blue Cheese-Onion Tart, 88
Crab Quiche, 51
Cranberry-Pear Pie, 80
French Apple Cream Pie, 71
Ginger-Scented Fig Tart, 142
Nectarine-Blueberry Pie, 127
Nutty Raisin Cream Pie, 79
Orchard Pear Tart, 82, 69
Pork-Spinach Pie, 52
Southwestern Quiche, 54
Sweet Potato Pie with Eggnog and Brandy, 75
Tangy Lemon Tart, 142
Wisconsin Cheese Pie, 78
Pimiento Spread, 43

Pineapple
Gingerberry Relish, 125
Southern Ambrosia, 16
Poinsettia-Shape Fruit Bread, 127, *117*
Poires Belle Hélène, 82, 83
Polenta Cheese Circles, 90
Pork
Apple-Stuffed Pork Loin, 13, *7*
Glazed Baked Ham, 14
Homemade Chorizo, 55
Pork-Spinach Pie, 52
Skillet Migas, 54
Spicy Pork Tenderloin with Lime Mayonnaise, 134
Potatoes
Blue Baked Potatoes, 92
Gruyère-Garlic Mashed Potatoes, 137
Heavenly Potatoes, 21
Potatoes Anna, 138
Potato-Parsnip Puree, 21
Slow-Cooker Holiday Potatoes, 25
Smoked Salmon Chowder, 10
The Ultimate Scalloped Potatoes, 22
Poultry *(see Chicken and Turkey)*
Praline-Yam Casserole, 23
Quaker Bonnet Biscuits, 60
Quesadillas, Smoked Trout, 35
Queso Fundido with Corn Bread Dippers, 44
Quiches
Crab Quiche, 51
Southwestern Quiche, 54
Raisins
Almond-Raisin Butter, 121
Cranberry Conserve, 124
Fruit and Nut Cheesecake Bars, 107
Lady Baltimore Cookies, 100
Nutty Raisin Cream Pie, 79
Poinsettia-Shape Fruit Bread, 127, *117*
Relishes
Cranberry Conserve, 124
Cranberry-Kumquat Relish, 13
Gingerberry Relish, 125
Rice
Cheesy Wild Rice Casserole, 19
Slow-Cooker Creamy Wild Rice Pilaf, 24
Stuffed Leg of Lamb, 14
Wild Rice Rolls, 66, 67
Royal Icing, 149
Rub, Spicy Barbecue, 121
Rum Filling, 105
Rum-Glazed Short Ribs with Figs, 134, *129*

S

Salads
Asparagus Salad with Tarragon Vinaigrette, 133
Baby Greens Salad with Oranges and Olives, 133
Creamy Cranberry Salad, 17
Hickory Nut Salad with Apples, 9
Southern Ambrosia, 16
Texas Red Grapefruit Salad, 16
Tossed Greens with Goat Cheese Phyllo Packets, 132
Warm Goat Cheese Salad, 90
Winter Fruit Cup, 53